How to Get and Keep
A GOOD MAN

Hope you· enJoy it!!!! visit ME onliNe at www.GetagoodmAN.com

Best,

How to Get and Keep
A GOOD MAN

From Successfully Single
to Happily Married

Alex B. Wright

iUniverse, Inc.
New York Lincoln Shanghai

How to Get and Keep A Good Man
From Successfully Single to Happily Married

iUniverse books may be ordered through booksellers or by contacting:

iUniverse
2021 Pine Lake Road, Suite 100
Lincoln, NE 68512
www.iuniverse.com
1-800-Authors (1-800-288-4677)

Design by Chandra Guglik

ISBN: 978-0-595-36518-0 (pbk)
ISBN: 978-0-595-84277-3 (cloth)
ISBN: 978-0-595-80952-3 (ebk)

Printed in the United States of America

I want to take the time to dedicate this book to my awesome and wonderful mom who I love more than I can express with words. Also my twin sisters; Norma who bought me my first laptop as a kid so I could begin writing, and Norine who continually encouraged as well as held me responsible for being a good man. I have to also thank my four other sisters who continually bless my life with love and support in so many different ways. My two daughters, and of course my beautiful wife who I love very much. Although I can't name every name, I do want to take the time to thank every woman that has been a part of my life in a great or a small way, because they all have effected me and have been a part of making me who I am to this day. To everyone I named and did not name I want say thank you, and I love you.

Contents

Preface

If you truly desire a deep, meaningful relationship filled with love, trust, and companionship, you can have one. That comment sounds pretty simple, right? If life was that easy, I guess I would have never been inspired to share this book with you. Building a quality relationship is much like other experiences in our lives. The experience will be great, but getting there can be frustrating and difficult.

You may have dreamed of discovering a secret list of how-tos for developing the right relationship and finding the right man. But, unlike the printed instructions you can use to put together a new desk that you have just bought, relationship instructions do not come with each individual man. To make things finding your perfect man even more difficult, there are different types of men, and no two relationships are alike.

So let's get the truth of this book out in the open very early. *How to Get and Keep a Good Man* will not perpetuate myths about dating rules or successful dating strategies or anything along those lines. Such myths may be fun to read, but the results of reading material that simplifies the most important elements of life and of relationships are usually far from ideal. People are individuals with feelings, emotions, backgrounds, and issues. If all we needed was a set of steps or rules for a successful relationship, then bad relationships probably wouldn't exist.

Relationships are a part of life, and they can be complex and have many levels that are not always clear to us. Just like all excellent parts of life, a successful relationship takes a certain amount of hard work, dedication, and sacrifice. If you desire a successful relationship and are willing to confront some of the most important, delicate emotions and situations in your life, then this book was written specifically for you. You will be able to fulfill the desires of your heart, and move forward in creating the best reality for your life long after you have forgotten you ever read this book. The ability to get and keep a good man lies within you. What we will do together as you read on is uncover the wonderful qualities you already have.

Introduction

"Always have enough money for carfare." My mother would repeat this sentence like a broken record any time one of my six sisters was getting ready to go out of our house on a date. My mother's reason for giving that advice was that if ever a date went wrong, my sisters could leave and get home safely on her own. This advice makes sense enough for me to tell my daughters when they start dating.

The inspiration to write this book came from a number of sources, all of them female. My experience with six sisters, two daughters, a wife, and a mother have shown me the importance of good relationships with good men, and those women are some of the most important reasons that I am willing to reveal many of the delicate secrets and issues that I have faced over the years. My family has always included a large number of females, and as a young man growing up in New York City; I also had a hefty portion of dealing with women from many different cultures and backgrounds.

One of my favorite experiences was working for a chain of stores called Lonny's, which sold stylish, very expensive women's clothing. Celebrities and models frequented our stores, which were located in the best neighborhoods in the city. On my way to or from work, I would bump into celebrities such as Madonna and Sean Penn, or I would sometimes have coffee standing with Sigourney Weaver near Gray's Papaya (a famous NYC hot dog spot).

Working at Lonny's for six years was a valuable experience, but the best part of the job was spending time with all the women I worked with. I was the only male, surrounded by women all day. It was great. For six years, I must have read every woman's magazine published and heard every form of complaint that a woman could make about men—husbands, ex-husbands, boyfriends, brothers-in-law, fathers, fathers new girlfriends etc … These complaints came not just from my female co-workers, but also from the female customers. After hearing those complaints all day, I went home to my six sisters (at times I thought I was living a cursed existence.). "All Girls: All the Time" was my life's radio station.

Yet after meeting a wonderful woman, getting married to her, and having two lovely daughters, I realized that those experiences of being around women were all a gift to me. Growing up surrounded by women was part of my life's purpose. I was born to write this book and to share my experiences and understanding with my readers. When my inspirations and experience meet your expectations, part of my purpose in life will be fulfilled. So as you read this book, you and I together will be participating in each other's destiny. I am looking forward to sharing parts of my life and experiences with you.

Although I'm sure that many ideas in this book will encourage and inspire you, I am equally sure that many of the book's concepts will challenge you and make you quite uncomfortable, even upset. Those negative feelings are part of the growth you can experience. Some parts of life are not pleasant, but if we're going to make the most of life, we have to experience those parts.

In writing this book, one commitment that I made to myself was that I would be honest with myself and honest with you. At times, though, being honest is like telling someone they have an unpleasant item in their nose. You don't want to tell the person that truth, but telling the person is a whole lot better than letting the person walk around looking like that. Being honest is a little easier for me because when you're reading this book, only you and I are involved in it. No one is around listening to what is going on inside you while you're experiencing the ideas I've written about. Reading this book can be a perfect opportunity for you to deal with some emotional issues that you may never have confronted with your friends, your family, or other people in your life. I'm glad you chose to take this journey with me. So now that you have been prepared, get ready for the adventure of a lifetime, and turn the page.

1

Relational Shadows

SHADOWS ARE DARK AREAS THAT TRAIL BEHIND OR beside us when we are blocking the light. Shadows may or may not be as spooky as they can be in the movies, but shadows can hold weight in our lives. If we don't shed light on our shadows, they will follow us around and haunt us forever. We'll start our journey by looking at a few shadows that previous relationships may have left behind in our lives.

It wouldn't be fair for you to embark on this journey completely alone, so I'll go with you. I won't have a chance to read any of your painful experiences, but you will have a chance to read a few of mine. I don't want to ask you to open up and share your experiences without sharing some of my own experiences first.

My story begins with my mom and dad. During all of my years growing up, I never saw my parent's kiss, hug, or show any type of affection toward one another. I am the youngest of eight children. Being the last child of six girls and two boys (my brother is 13 years older than I am) was not easy. When I was four years old, my older brother left for the Army, so I was left in the house with seven women and my dad. That sounds like a nightmare for a young boy, but I had a very strong and strict mother who instilled values in me values and gave me the space to learn to be a man.

My dad was also an integral part of my life. He was the role model and the provider. I grew up in a four-bedroom house with a second floor and an *almost* finished basement. There were three bedrooms upstairs, and my parents slept in the bedroom downstairs. One day when I was about five years old, my mom and dad were arguing loudly while my sisters and I were upstairs. We listened intently as their argument seemed to be much worse than usual. As the youngest, I understood the least about what was going on.

At last my dad in anger and frustration vowed to leave the house. He had packed his bags and was on his way out. Suddenly, as I realized that my dad—the only other male in my house—was really leaving, I rushed down the stairs in fear and panic. My dad was not only the only man in my life, but my dad was my hero, my world. He wasn't just a man to me, but; he was "The Man". The man that every man should be, the man that I was going to be but only better, and now he was leaving forever. My heart was racing as I ran downstairs, desperately trying to catch him before he left. With the vision in my mind of the door slamming in my face and my father being gone, I reached the bottom of the stairs and saw my father carrying his bags on the way to the front door.

There was no way he was going to leave now, I thought to myself. I ran to him, grabbed his legs, and squeezed them as tightly as I could. I began screaming, "Daddy, please don't go! Daddy, please don't go!"

As I despondently squeezed the legs of the most important man in my life, I cried like never before. You see, as a five year old my father was my world, and there's no greater feeling than when the world is in your hands. Unfortunately, although fairy tales have happy endings, my story was no fairy tale, and my father peeled me off his leg and left me there crying on the floor.

In all my life, I had never felt emotional pain like that. I stayed on the floor, crying after the door closed, before I began to realize that my dad wasn't going to turn around and walk back inside. To make the experience worse, when I finally pulled myself up from the floor to go back upstairs to my room, I was met by two of my sisters, who began to make fun of me. Imitating my cries and desperate pleas, they heckled me all the way upstairs until I reached my room. When I was a five-year-old child, my parents made decisions that created emotional scars and anger that tumbles around in my heart until this very day.

My father's departure was one of the dark places in my life, one of my Shadows of Life. Such life events that create our personal Shadows of life are the memories we must visit in order to prepare ourselves for successful relationships. We must visit these dark places that are hidden deep inside our minds and expose them to the light of truth and reality. Only then will the scabs fall from our emotional wounds to reveal us as brand-new, healed, and unscarred persons.

Now that I've told you about one of my Shadows of Life, it's your turn to revisit your Shadows of Life. I have shared one of my stories with you, and now we can walk through your stories together. Tell the story of the first extremely painful experience in your life that pertains to your father. If you have never known your father, then speak about some of the thoughts you have had concerning him as an absent parent. Describe how you may have felt neglected or alone. Explain your feelings of being unwanted or your conclusions that men can't be trusted. Take the time to write about any and every feeling you've had concerning your father or your father figure. This first opportunity for sharing also doesn't just have to be about your father. It can be another male family member that may have hurt you someway as well.

I'd like for you to grab your companion diary or journal, and let those painful memories inside of you flow out onto the pages. Write and share your experiences with the two most important people in your life, yourself and God. Speak to yourself and to him as you share the most painful experiences and disappointments in your life concerning your father. Don't procrastinate; start writing right away. When you're done, come back to the next paragraph.

Now that you've written about your feelings and thoughts, take a moment to pray or meditate, or do what it is that you do that can help you. If you don't have anything that you do, I suggest that you pray and talk to God as though he is your best friend. It is important that you express yourself spiritually after dealing with important issues in your life. This will help you as you make the transition from dealing with pain from the past to present every day life. Take a few moments to do so, and then go on to the next paragraph.

That painful experience that I shared with you caused me to make a very important decision. At the age of five, I decided that no matter what happened in my life or my marriage, I would never leave my children, no matter what the circumstances. Even though I didn't know what it meant to be married and have children, I knew that whatever it meant I wasn't going to leave.

Many times we underestimate the will and the understanding of a child. As you visit your painful memories and begin to discover who you really are, you are likely to find that much of who you are as a person has been shaped and molded by the experiences you had and the decisions you made during your childhood and adolescent years.

Fortunately, the decision I made never to leave my children was a positive result of a negative circumstance, and that decision has stuck with me for the rest of my life. From this painful experience I was able to pull out positive results that committed me forever to my children as a father. What is a positive decision that you have made, or would like to make, as a result of the experience you just shared? Don't write the first decision you remember making, but try to find a positive decision that you may have made as a result of your experience. You can share the way you try to treat people in a certain situation, or you can write about how you try to approach a certain issue or situation. Or you may choose to write about a concrete, positive decision that you made after your experience. Take a moment to think about this subject, and write your decisions down. Knowing the choices and the decisions you have made will help you a great deal as we go through our shadows together. Take a moment to visit your decisions, and see what you come up with. If you are comfortable with it then feel free to write them down in your companion journal or diary. If not take a few moments and then move on.

My decision to be a committed father was unfortunately not the only decision I made on the day my father left. In addition to the one positive decision I made, I made many more conscious and unconscious decisions as a result of that painful event. Some of my decisions that resulted from my father's departure were very negative.

That day I also decided that I was going to hate forever those two sisters who teased me. I vowed never to be like them or anyone else in my family. I also decided that I would always keep my feelings to myself forever. I believed those feelings would never be valuable to anyone and that no one would ever appreciate them. The honest expression of my true feelings had failed at that moment when my father left. I felt it was obvious that my dad didn't appreciate my feelings and that my sisters didn't either, so why would anybody else care about me if my own flesh and blood didn't care?

I hurt inside the day my father left, and all of my decisions stayed with me like a heavy ball and chain. I carried that weight for years, dragging down my heart and my life. I felt miserable about my father and my family for many years before I was finally set free from the weight of my decisions.

Many people walk around carrying weights like mine. Many books, magazine articles, and people encourage others to keep their heavy weights clanging about them and to accept them. Over time, I have realized that life is not meant to be spent carrying huge emotional weights that can negatively affect our everyday relationships. Those weights can be detrimental to successful living, for they are an unconscious and unpleasant form of bondage.

Can you feel heavy weights on your heart from your past experiences and feelings? Feelings of bitterness, fear, anger? The positive decision or decisions that you wrote down are probably not the only ones you made as a result of experience that you have shared. What are some of the poor decisions that you made as a result of that experience? Take a few minutes to pray or do what it is you do, and then share those poor decisions by writing them in your journal or diary. Also, share the feelings that still stir inside you when you think about those poor decisions. If you don't pray or meditate, I suggest that now may be a good time to give these activities a try.

⤳

Your willingness to share your thoughts and experiences in your journal or diary during this journey is very important to you.

We all have shadows in our lives that we need to shed some light on, and it's important we know that we are not the only ones with baggage. If you like, you may want to take a few minutes or maybe a day before you continue to the next part of your journey. Rest your heart before we move on to the next turn on our journey.

2

Where Am I Going?

WHAT IS THE RIGHT ADVICE, FORMULA, TECHNIQUE, or lucky charm that will help you find the man of your dreams? Books, magazine articles, friends, relatives, and other people who do not know how to mind their own business are all very quick to give advice on relationships between men and women. How can you tell which advice is right? Is it the advice that makes you feel good about yourself? Is it the advice that makes you feel bad? Or is it the advice that confirms something that you already believe? There are so many answers to so many questions that it's hard to determine which are the right ones.

Figuring out what direction to take in any important aspect of life can be exhausting. It would be much easier if someone could just list the steps to take so that we could take them. I won't give you a list to check off, and I won't give you a set of rules follow. I will share with you stories, situations, and circumstances that can encourage and enlighten you about men and relationships. This book was written for every daughter, every mom, every sister, every wife, and you. If you are reading this book right now, it is not an accident; it is a part of your destiny. However it happened you have this book in your hand right now, and your life may be about to change.

A successful relationship in today's world is a bit uncommon. In order to develop a successful relationship, you need views, actions, and expectations that are equally uncommon. Having a high quality, long-lasting, and fulfilling relationship has very little to do with you finding the right man and much more to do with finding the right mind in yourself. As you begin to develop the right mind, the right man will find you.

As you take this journey seriously, you will have some experiences by yourself. Relationships are personal, and this journey is also very personal. If you are serious about the relationships or the desired relationships in your life, you must be a solitary learner. I will be your guide, but you are the hero.

2. Where Am I Going?

If you scribble on or write in this book while you are reading and thinking about it, you should probably not lend the book to a friend or leave the book lying around unattended. This book is yours. It will contain a record of your private experiences, thoughts and emotions. The ideas that will challenge you in this book will be extremely emotional and personal, but can also be very beneficial.

In order for us to be ful-*filled*, sometimes we must first be emptied out. This journey will guide you through of the processes of cleansing and healing, and onward from there toward a fulfilling relationship. You will need only a few key things to successfully complete this journey: a journal or diary, a pen, time, and a life that is ready for change.

3

Where Are You?

GETTING TO KNOW YOURSELF IS ONE OF THE MOST important aspects of life. Yet we all avoid it really knowing ourselves. Maybe it is to protect us from dealing with the unpleasant things in our lives that are essentially our fault. Yet ignoring parts of our lives and personalities that aren't the most flattering is a major cause of self-sickness, and issues in relating to others consistently on a long-term basis. We often give in to our weaknesses and allow them to become strongholds in our lives. As a result, we may develop a very typical attitude that is a combination of insecurity and low self-esteem. This particular type of attitude is what I call "Self-sickness." Self-sickness is a constant comparison of yourself to others, which results in parts of your self that make you sick. This constantly will affect an individual's confidence and comfort level with themselves, and often leads to a consistency in broken and bad relationships. A woman who has "self-sickness" avoids dealing with the shortcomings that make her life unnecessarily hard, and doesn't address the good in her own life, which would enable her life to get even better. Unconsciously or consciously she may know this, and it results in a loss of willpower, and the confidence to stick to good but hard decisions in her life.

Capitalism has profited from self-sickness by offering many treatments such as breast implants and breast augmentation, face lifts, tummy tucks, a host of diet pills, exercise machines, and more. All these commercial products are usually only beneficial to those that sell them. You might think of them as band-aids on bullet wounds because they address only the symptoms, and side effects of self-sickness. They zero in on the negative effects of self sickness and offer products that provide temporary emotional boost, but in the long term can damage a woman's self esteem, confidence and ability to have long lasting quality relationships.

Our society and media specifically indicate certain types of women and designate them as beautiful. This consistently reinforces and perpetuates self-sickness because it gives a narrow view of the true beauty of a woman, and making it appear to the masses that attractive women only look or have bodies that are a certain way. Although those ridiculous conceptions are very far from the truth, they affect our culture in an enormous way. Women who don't look "beautiful" according to the specifications of society and the media may are very prone to actually feel less beautiful or less valuable. It can cause a loss of self-esteem, confidence and an overall feeling of being sexy. These simple things can become critical over time in a relationship and if they are not dealt with can destroy a relationship that may have worked wonderfully otherwise. Please bear with me as I am trying to express the important role that these issues play in a relationship. I desire for you to understand that the success of your present and future relationships have a great deal to do with your willingness to confront and deal with any form of self-sickness in your life. It can make the difference between a lasting wonderful and fulfilling relationship, and a horrible break-up or divorce.

Consistent random dissatisfaction, frustration, anger and anxiety are common symptoms of self-sickness. Thus self-sickness affects not only your ability to have quality relationships with men, but also can affect the delicate relationship between you and your boss, your children, and any other male or female in your life. Many women are the daughters of women who have suffered from this condition, so that in a sense self-sickness can also becomes socially inherited.

Women who have experienced consistent unsuccessful relationships could have this issue based on the relationships that her mother or father has had with each other or others. We will deal with much of this in this chapter and begin to uncover what the potential issue or issues (if any) may be, and deal with them immediately.

The answers we need to seek in this part of the journey are the following:

- Do you, and to what extent do you suffer from self-sickness?
- How do your past's emotional wounds affect your everyday attitude and behavior in relationships?

This is a part of your journey that is very personal. In a few moments you will write about the feelings you've never shared and the places in your heart that you don't visit because doing so may be too painful. Those are the places where you have perhaps hidden the pain and fear of not measuring up to what society and the media have specified as beautiful. You can write of an event or multiple events that have happened in your recent past or your childhood. Anything in your life that is so emotionally painful that you try to block it out. These are so of the places we must go on the next part of our journey together.

Grab all of the necessary tools: a pen or pencil and your journal or diary, as well as uninterrupted time. You may have to turn off your cell phone, your computer, and all other ways that people can contact or distract you. Then prepare your heart to empty itself of lifelong burdens.

Now share in your journal one of the most emotionally painful experiences in your life, and also what are some of the changes in your life and personality since then as a result of it. When you are done have something warm or cool to drink dependant upon your feelings at that moment. Then take a break and begin reading the next section tomorrow.

⌒

Take a moment to think about what you are looking forward to getting out of reading this book. It may have already changed since you first picked it up. Think about what you feel you may get out of it now, and how it has changed since your first impression. Be honest. If you get a chance write it down in your journal the next time you have it close by. At the end of your journey inside this book revisit what you have written to see whether or not your expectations have been met. What you receive from reading this book is very important to me, and I would love to hear your thoughts and feelings about it.

4

Cleaning the Wounds

NOW THAT WE HAVE OPENED UP AND SHARED OUR past wounds, let's clean them out so they can heal properly this time without any scars. We will take a look at some of the less positive decisions we have made as a result of our painful childhood experiences with our father or other people in our lives.

In life it is always easy to tear things apart and break them down, but it is much harder to put things back together. It is the same way with people. It can be easy to lash out and hurt someone, but much harder to heal those painful wounds. I think this is especially true when the wounds involve emotions and relationships. Sticks and stones may break your bones but words can never hurt you. That sounds good, but like many false proverbs it is very far from the truth. The reality of that popular saying is "sticks and stones may break your bones but words can ruin up your life!" Healing from emotional wounds is difficult. Our society has in turn made it acceptable for us to keep those wounds and to hide them. We cover our emotional wounds and our painful baggage with drinking, drug use, sex, work, reclusive behavior, excuses, and a host of other well-thought-out cover-ups. The problem is that a cover-up doesn't heal a wound. Once our wounds are exposed—and in most relationships, they will eventually become exposed—those wounds begin to reveal the damage that made them. As a result, unhealed wounds can destroy or severely damage relationships and families, leaving them with even more wounds and painful baggage than they had before.

The key to finding and keeping a wonderful, lasting relationship in your life is your ability to heal your emotional wounds and take control over your own destiny. Regardless of the emotional and relational scars and wounds that you have, you can change your life. Whether or not you have been or still are in a failed relationship, you have a chance for your life to be different and better.

Loneliness and an empty heart, covered up with a nice smile and a pleasant face, is not part of your destiny. The fact that you are reading this book indicates that you have chosen a different path for yourself. By your effort, this path will not be associated with the status quo of the society or people that surround you. You are destined for something better. It doesn't sound real does it? That word—destiny. I don't want you to confuse fate with destiny. Fate is a belief that your life has a predetermined course, but destiny is a choice. It is something you have to fulfill and participate in. Your destiny has joy, love, acceptance and satisfaction if you choose to fulfill it. Destiny is positive or negative results based on the actions you take in life. Fulfill your destiny of being adored and loved, as you desire. Make quality choices and decisions. Take responsibility for yourself and your relationships.

Being close to true joy and happiness can be a little frightening. Your destination of finding a loving, satisfying, and fulfilling relationship awaits your arrival. Just remember, arriving at this destination is a result of choices you make and actions you take.

As you move toward your desired destination, you may find that you will have to leave some ideas and understandings behind and that you will keep others. All of the places you have been are parts of the voyage that we call life. Some roads were pleasant, some horrifying. Some roads you came across by good choices and some by bad ones, and some you had no choice at all in the matter. Yet all of these roads both pleasant and unpleasant make you the wonderful person you are, and the even better person you will become. The popular phrase "Life sucks and then you die" is for people who have camped out at a bad road on their journey, not wanting change in their lives enough to keep walking. Your destiny has led you to this book, so lets and walk towards your future … one step at a time. Now once again is the time to get out all of the necessary tools for your journey. You cannot be around anyone at this time, or on a bus or a train or any public place. This is a road you must travel with only you and God.

The first step in cleansing our wounds and moving forward on our journey is that dreadful word that may spring up cynicism, anger and bitterness at the very thought of it. This word can create a pocket in your heart where you store past pain and replace it with a smile on your face that really says, "this sucks but I'm going to suck it up like everybody else." This word, or rather action that we may talk about but hardly practice is called forgiveness.

That word put into action can really appear tough if not impossible hurt sometimes if we take it seriously. Forgiving those who have hurt us may seem difficult or even impossible, but what can really hurt you is not allowing the power of forgiveness to flow freely through your life. Sometimes we tell ourselves, "I'll forgive, but I won't forget" when we are faced with a situation that calls for forgiveness. What we really are saying is, "I'm watching you, and I will not trust you or anybody else with my feelings or my life in that way any more." Sometimes we allow the pain from being hurt by someone to extend further to include other people, and many say you can't trust anyone.

At its very core, the mindset that refuses to trust others or to have faith in others is the opposite of forgiveness. The dilemma is that in order for us to forgive someone completely, we have to allow ourselves to become vulnerable again and to let our fear and need to be loved and appreciated become exposed. We have to accept of the fact that everybody who lives on this earth has the same need to forgive and to be forgiven. There is no reason for us to be ashamed or to feel insecure about our forgiveness needs and our needs to be loved, understood and appreciated. When you understand those very important needs, you can begin to move on in your healing process. Just like a real flesh wound, an emotional scar must be revealed in order for it to heal.

To truly forgive someone is to say that you will give that person the opportunity to hurt you again *and* to, believe and trust in your heart that you won't be hurt again. Allowing yourself to be vulnerable and exposed is extremely difficult and frightening. Yet you must allow yourself to trust and to be vulnerable with someone you love, not so that people can step on you or abuse you, but so that you can be free.

One hurtful person does not represent everyone in the world, yet we carry emotional baggage from one relationship to the other as if what happens in one relationship must apply to every relationship. That feeling has to be let go! You can conquer your painful past and live a life free of issues that may have prevented you from forming a good lasting relationships. You have to surrender your pride, surrender your guilt, surrender your emotional defenses, and allow people into your heart and into your life.

Is that too much to expect? Did you say to yourself, "I can't do that?" I know I said that when I was first faced with the reality of true forgiveness and openness to others. My stomach twisted into knots at the thought of having to revisit people or situations that had hurt me, especially when I knew I'd have to turn in my badge of pride and give those people the opportunity to hurt me again. My first thought to myself was "Never!" Yet the only medicine that truly heals emotional scars and pain is the soothing balm of love and forgiveness.

To continue on your journey of healing and self-knowledge, please follow these two steps.

4. Cleaning the Wounds

STEP ONE

Please write in your diary or journal the names of three people who have hurt you deeply, either when you were a child or when you were an adult. You might choose to include your father in this list if you wrote about him during the last written part of our journey.

After you have written the names, try writing a brief story that shares your painful experiences with the first person and explain how that experience made you feel. Then write some words that express feelings that you may have felt and maybe still feel as a result of those experiences. Repeat this for each person.

It's time to put your desire to change into action. I cannot stress enough how much you need to be alone right now, in a place where people cannot hear you or disturb you. It doesn't matter how well you write, just take the time to express yourself and your feelings.

Finish your writing, and then go on to the next section.

STEP TWO

Focus on the first person you named on your list, and think about how the person hurt you and how you felt. In as loud a voice as you wish, audibly scream out to that person how much you were hurt, and how they made you feel. Although you are alone, talk to that person and say, "You hurt me!"

When you are ready, scream out to the person again, "I forgive you for _____." Fill in the blank by describing what the person did to hurt you.

It is important that you scream loudly to the people that hurt you and release the build up inside of you. This will help free yourself of these past feelings that have put chains on your life. You must get these things out of your soul and out of your life. Scream out and free yourself once and for all, scream out and forgive them. After you have dealt an individual person take a moment to sit down and have a cup of tea, hot chocolate, or a glass of water before going on with the rest of your day.

You may also want to take some time before you continue the healing process by screaming out to the other two people on your list. This process can be very emotional and tiring. I suggest that you deal with only one person on your list a day. So take two more days to completely finish this part of your journey.

If you have finished screaming out words of anger and forgiveness in order to cleanse yourself, move on to Step Three. If not, be sure you finish this exercise before moving on. Remember that this important journey can and will change your life if you let it.

Do not move on until you have dealt completely with these painful issues in your heart. Get the full value of your journey. Do Step One completely, and move toward your freedom now.

STEP THREE

Find a quiet place where you can be alone and make a list of three to five people you love, and or have loved, in order of most influential in your life. After your list is made kneel down and quietly ask for forgiveness for ways you may have hurt them knowingly and unknowingly. If you feel that it will be best to tell the person that you are sorry face to face then by all means do that. Just make sure that doing so is not dangerous. I am sorry for _____. Forgive me if I hurt you by _____. Those are examples of things that you need to fill in the blanks for. You may have other things to say as well and please feel free to say them. It is just as important for you to allow yourself to be forgiven, and to forgive yourself for things you may have done. Do not allow yourself to be defined by an individual action or a past way of living. Ask for your forgiveness and free yourself of some of the hidden burdens you may carry because of what you may have done to others. Take at least two days to do this, and then move on to part four.

STEP FOUR

After you have cleansed yourself of the pain that was inside you, you must refill that space in your mind and heart with feelings and knowledge that can keep you on the right path to peace. For this part of our journey, you may have to step into a bathroom or a place with a mirror so that you can look at your face. This exercise will probably be even more uncomfortable than the first exercise, but the results can be even better.

While looking at yourself in the mirror, say each sentence loud and clear.

1. I am valuable.
2. I am worthwhile.
3. I am important.
4. I am loved.
5. I am tender.
6. I am beautiful.
7. In my future, there is joy.

Although you may not now be in the situation or circumstance that you wish to be in, you still have the power and the resources to change. Strength and hope equal power. No matter how tiny your combination if those attributes are, the fact that you have even a small amount gives you power. If you have done these exercises, you have used a small amount of your power to make your life better.

If you have more names of people on the list that you wrote down earlier, go through this exercise again. Then you'll be ready to move on!

5

The Ghosts of Relationships Past

MEN AND WOMEN THINK, RESPOND, AND REACT differently to different things. Men and women have different needs as well, but both sexes want intimate, loving relationships. They want someone they can trust, rely on, talk to, and be both physically and emotionally connected to.

If both sexes do want such relationships, why are there so many broken relationships and scarred people? Why are many men viewed as dogs, and why are many women viewed as victims? Clearly somewhere along the line there is a breakdown in the understanding of relationships between men and women.

To understand how this failure of understanding happens, let's look at the very first relationship of a typical young girl and how it affected her then and continues to affect her adult life. This is a true story, so of course all names and locations have been changed.

Jennifer was a very attractive sixteen-year-old who lived in the Upper West Side of Manhattan. With a beautiful face, lovely skin, and a relatively voluptuous but slim body, Jennifer was one of the most sought-after girls in her neighborhood. Early in her life she realized that many men, both old and young, would continually be attracted to her. She was never interested or attracted to any of them, and she saw no future with any of the young or old men that were interested in her. She was young, beautiful and innocent at the time.

Jennifer was about to turn seventeen and began to feel very lonely and displaced in her family. Her desire for a meaningful relationship began to grow into an emotional need. Unfortunately, there were no neighborhood or high school guys who interested her except one who already had a girlfriend. So Jennifer spent time with her girlfriends from school, and her childhood friends from her area.

One day a young man, Ron, who was in college, came back to the neighborhood for vacation. All of the neighborhood girls thought he was very hot, including Jennifer. He also represented what almost every girl in the neighborhood wanted. He was good-looking and obviously successful. He drove a convertible, attended a great college and every girl he was seen with was absolutely stunning. Something about Ron just made women smile when they say him. As if they were looking at some sort of dream. When Jennifer turned seventeen, Ron finally noticed her among all of the other pretty girls. Seeing her at a local party, Ron invited the beautiful but insecure young Jennifer to the movies and dinner. Ron's experience and his looks were no match for Jennifer's innocence. In a few weeks dinner was followed by the life-changing loss of Jennifer's virginity. Feeling fearful and disappointed after this event, she protected emotions with her blissful thought that she would marry Ron one day, and that they both loved each other very much.

That date was followed with a stream of calls and dates with Ron, that all ended in sex. Ron continually told Jennifer how beautiful and wonderful she was and how much he loved her while they were together. He would consistently make her feel momentarily wonderful about life, and about herself when they were together, but soon the reality of the shallow relationship that he offered her began to take it's toll.

Jennifer still felt lonely and even more insecure because Ron didn't spend much time with her except just before sex. He told her weekends were his time to spend with the guys, and during the week he spent most of his time working. As he explained it, the short time that he did have he wanted to be with her. In the car, on the beach or when no one was home would all be intimate sexual time together. He made her feel special and important during the brief time they were together, he even bought her a few gifts, and from the eyes of most of the other young girls around her—Jennifer had made it.

Unfortunately, Jennifer was soon devastated to find out that she was pregnant. Her family was equally upset and demanded that she have an abortion, and Ron echoed their opinion. Everyone said that the abortion would be best for both of him and her futures. But Jennifer disagreed because she felt that having the baby was the right thing to do and that the baby shouldn't suffer because of its parents' poor decisions. Jennifer also hoped that the baby would solve many of her emotional and relational problems. She would no longer be lonely all the time and would always have someone who loved her and would always need her. She thought to herself that Ron was a good guy with a future and that he would ask to marry her if she actually decided to have the baby.

Jennifer spent time daydreaming about shopping for the baby with Ron, having picnics with the baby and Ron, and enjoying a happy and loving family. She didn't understand why Ron wasn't supportive about having his own baby. Even though he said he would be there for her, he constantly pressed her to get an abortion.

Jennifer had wonderful and understandable hopes and dreams, yet they were not to be realized. She gave birth to the baby, a beautiful girl named Tyler, with little involvement from Ron. After the baby's birth, he made minimal attempts to spend time with his daughter unless a nightcap was involved in the meeting. Shortly after her birth Ron was soon nowhere to be found.

Jennifer is now twenty-six years old and has a seven-year-old daughter who barely knows her father. Jennifer hasn't had a serious relationship since her relationship with Ron, and any time she enters into a relationship, it ends very shortly. Again she is left empty and alone, feeling that she is going to be single forever. She is still attractive, but every year her beauty fades, and she believes that her chances of finding a mate grow slimmer every day, and are magnified because she already has a child. Her fears and beliefs are justified, but very far from the truth. If Jennifer continues on her current path she will eventually become a destined single: An attractive young woman that strangely no man desires to have a relationship with. Jennifer went from living out a dream to living out a nightmare. Her first relationship left scars that can affect every potential relationship in her future if she does not deal with the reality of her relational scars.

Jennifer's relationship experience is very common. In many instances it is not as dramatic. Many women protect themselves from pregnancy or have abortions and eventually move on to other relationships. When the relationships end, the relational and emotional damage follows and puts many women in the position to ruin every future relationship or potential relationship. The lives of these women have been put on pause because they repeat the same unsuccessful scenarios with different people, and the result is always the same—a failed relationship.

Usually the damage created in previous relationships consistently affects every relationship that follows. Yet in severe cases, relational paralysis can occur is so damaging that many women unconsciously destroy every opportunity for a lasting and meaningful relationship. In the essence of their realities the understanding of men that they hold on to dates back to their teenage years, and they have never confronted or dealt with their issues since. It becomes normal and acceptable to live with inner frustration, loneliness and disenchantment with relationships altogether. Keep in mind that everyone experiences relational problems that effect how he or she feels about themselves and others. The key is not allowing our problems to steer your personality, and in turn your future.

Jennifer made critical mistakes in her relationship with Ron that she never has dealt with. She continually blames her situation on his lack of a decent character and irresponsible and selfish attributes. Yes Ron treated Jennifer horribly, but Jennifer must take responsibility for her life and her decisions in order to successfully move on.

In your diary or journal, share your first serious boyfriend experience and do your best to answer each of these questions:

- What was your first serious boyfriend like?
- When it ended, how did you feel about yourself?
- How did you feel about the guy?
- How did you feel afterward about men in general?

After you're done sharing in your journal begin reading again from here.

Your relationship may or may not have been as bad as Jennifer's, or it may have been much more painful. Every relationship leaves emotional deposits, and bad relationships leave wounds that need to be opened and then healed. If we can deal with these painful experiences in our past, we can secure success for our relationships in the future. It's important for us to remember that Jennifer never realized that she had made crucial mistakes in that first relationship. By never dealing with her failure, she has her ability to have a successful relationship on pause. Jennifer's ideas about "who" men are is a common effect of not dealing with the residue of bad relationships.

This view is a very common and culturally accepted view of men. Yet when a woman views men in this way, her belief can be very damaging because it becomes a self-fulfilling prophecy. Many women who have that view as a base for their understanding of men tend to gravitate towards men who will treat them that way. Because on some level these women typically think that all a man wants is sex they never recognize and attend to the other needs that men have.

Jennifer agrees with the common belief that all men just want sex. Her relational experiences confirm this belief in her mind. Now she feels that if she can find a nice enough man who has a decent future and is interested in her, the next step is sex. After that he should have everything he wants because he likes her in the first place … right? Wrong! Nothing could be further from the truth. This false premise has put Jennifer in a state of relational pause until she comes to grips with her relational scars, accepts responsibility for her own situations, and receives forgiveness and healing from her emotional and rela- tional relationship wounds. Jennifer and many women like her must begin to take responsibility for their actions and forgive themselves. Jennifer must admit that regardless of how she may have felt, what she did in that relationship was a mistake. Accepting the situation as a mistake on her part empowers Jennifer to change her circumstances by correcting and learning from her those mistakes. Denying herself of being the cause of her own problems will paralyze Jennifer. She will forever believe that her life and relational circumstances are in the hands of someone else, or up to chance. If she does not deal with this, the ramifications can be devastating to her relational life. Potentially setting her self up for multiple failed relationships, and a prime candidate to unhappily single for the rest of her life.

- What mistakes may you have made during your failed relationship?
- Did you blame the man in the relationship for its failure?
- What will you do next time around to ensure you don't repeat the same mistakes?
- How will these changes help your next relationship to succeed?

Now you have shared some of your deepest, most intimate relationship thoughts and experiences and have heard the story of Jennifer's relationship mistakes. In the next chapter, we'll look at Jennifer's situation from a male perspective, and then we can understand how Jennifer moved from living her dream to experiencing a nightmare. Our exploration of her situation will allow you to look at your past experiences from a different angle and give you a greater understanding into the mind of a man.

6

How Men Think of Women

IF A WOMAN IS ATTRACTIVE AND INTELLIGENT, WHY is it difficult for her to find a good man? Are men intimidated by her success? Are all of the good men taken? Is no good man interested in a woman who has a child? All of those ideas are closer to being excuses than they are to being the truth. If a woman never understands how men view relationships and women, and if she fails to deal with the effects of her emotional and relationship wounds, she will grow old and gray trying to figure out the answer to those questions.

When the average man is at a strip club spending money, or when he is looking at porn for women he thinks are hot, he is not looking for a girlfriend or a wife. In spite of his actions and his references to the women, his mind is in another place. Whether men are dating or going out to clubs and parties, men organize women in their minds according to their desirable and undesirable attributes. Different women are placed in different categories for every man.

To understand what happened in Jennifer's life, you have to understand how men categorize women. This may sound a little coarse, but when I wrote this book I made a commitment to be honest, to give you the understanding that you need to get and maintain a successful relationship. With that said, lets dig into the mind of the male and see what comes up.

When a man finds a woman attractive an immediate mental response is made. Depending on what she is wearing and on the man's background, he immediately places her into one of only two categories: a woman he might want to marry, or a woman he would like to have sex with. The category assignment happens that fast. After the initial assumption, during the man's interaction with this woman is where the true categorization takes place. Is she a potential wife, or just potential sex? This is a key point that you must remember: *Sex and relationship are two very different and separate things in the life of a man.* If a man doesn't find a woman attractive initially, he has a totally different response, but for now let's stay with the situation of the woman who is found attractive.

Where did Jennifer go wrong? What took place that landed her in the wrong category and prevented her from developing a meaningful relationship with Ron?

Jennifer saw an opportunity for her dreams to come true, and although Ron appears to be a complete womanizer (and or dirt bag), in fact he is a very typical man. Ron *might* have been a good man for Jennifer. All of the potential for a lasting relationship was there before the relationship began. Key mistakes were made in the beginning that guaranteed that any potential relationship would be a failure. Jennifer had sex with Ron almost instantly, and as a result she represented neither an intellectual stimulus nor challenge to Ron. By having sex with Ron immediately, Jennifer also made it almost impossible for Ron ever to consider her as a potential wife. Even if at the beginning he saw her as wife material all of that flew out of the window after the immediate sex.

From a male perspective, Jennifer never had a boyfriend at all. Ron never considered himself her boyfriend or anything even remotely close. To Ron, she was a good-looking girl that he could have sex with whenever he wanted. Understand this: men will have sex with a woman he finds attractive even if he doesn't like her at all. I could even go as far as to say that even if the guy thinks the girl is a horrible person, he will might still have sex with her if he finds her remotely attractive.

Unfortunately, many women think that if a guy is flirting with her in a sexual or non-sexual way, he actually likes her as a person. Nothing could be further from the truth! This may make understanding men a bit difficult, but this is who we are. If Ron had really liked Jennifer in a relationship sense, he would have made opportunities to spend time with her, doing many things other than sex. He would have enjoyed her presence, planned ways to experience fun activities with her, introduced her to his family, and shared his intimate dreams, failures, and victories. This was far from the case.

Jennifer assumed that because he was calling often to see her, he genuinely liked her. She believed that if she gave him what every man wants, he would marry her. Her feelings in this situation are very understandable, and it hurts me to even share her story because I care about Jennifer and she is my friend. Jennifer wound up in the wrong category in Ron's mind, and their actions ruined any chance of a meaningful relationship between the two of them.

Good men need good, strong women. Men don't want women who are strong in a traditionally masculine way—that is, women who are stubborn, forceful, determined to get their way, and too proud to ask for directions. Good men need women who are strong in their femininity, their security about themselves, and their self-respect. A good man longs to find a woman who is not like a man at all, a woman who can walk beside him and help him to fulfill his destiny, and fulfills hers in the process. Good men are searching all over the place looking for you.

Another key point that you must understand about men is that they seek challenges and the opportunities to overcome them. When being in a relationship with a woman is not satisfying emotionally, having a relationship with her is not an option. Having sex with her is. Sex does not produce nor is a result of an emotional bond for men. Therefore, a relationship that is based solely on sex is not a relationship at all to a man. It is simply an opportunity for sex and nothing more.

This information may be a bit hard to accept, but it is the unadulterated truth about men. If you embrace it, you will be much more powerful than before. Jennifer didn't have anyone to teach her about men in this way, and she made crucial relationship errors that changed her life forever. Grab on to this information and engrave it in the forefront of your mind. As you do, it will give back to you years that you may have lost through decisions you made without it.

We all realize that today, a relationship is different from what it used to be. Yet I don't want to confuse women into thinking that their playing hard to get is a smart way to get or keep a good man, because it is not. Acting coy and playing hard to get in order to encourage a man to ask for a date is rarely if ever the right way to challenge a good man in today's society. Far more important is how you behave during and after that date. Jennifer's misunderstanding of the male mind was a reasonable but very harmful mistake. After the initial date Jennifer posed no relationship challenge or interest to Ron at all. Her virginity was lost along with all of her respect from Ron. This unfortunate and very common mistake doesn't make Jennifer out to be a whore or a slut even though many people may refer to her as such. It really just makes her a victim of an understandable bad decision.

We have all are victims of our own bad decisions in relationships. We must deal with and understand those decisions and work on not repeating our mistakes. Unless Jennifer and the many women like her deal with their past mistakes, they will consistently repeat their relationship errors and will live in frustration, loneliness, and confusion. If Jennifer could understand and overcome her mistake with Ron, she would no longer be a victim, but a conqueror.... A champion. But if she does not gain that understanding and take action to heal her emotional wounds, she is likely to find it very difficult if not impossible to find her Mr. Wright, her soul mate.

Jennifer's unfortunate encounters with Ron have crippled her in her adult life because based on her understanding she still feels as if she had a real relationship with Ron. This misunderstanding of the situation makes it very hard for her to relate with and develop a long-lasting relationship with a man who is actually interested in her. On some level, Jennifer expects other men to treat her similarly to the way Ron did. She will always have her experience with Ron in the back of her mind, and she will have the conclusions she has made drawn about men in her heart.

Jennifer is likely to feel that the results of her future relationships are determined by whether the man is a decent guy or not. Yet she will experience uncomfortable feelings with a man who wants to spend time talking to her or getting to know who she really is. He may even appear to be less masculine to her. Although she longs for an intimate and meaningful relationship, all of her understanding, feelings and actions may push her far away from her dreams.

Jennifer and many women like her must come to the realization that they bring and should bring much more than sex to a relationship. A good woman provides a good man with the security he needs to let down his guard and become vulnerable and sensitive, without running the risk of losing his masculinity or his respect as a man. Such a man and such a woman can develop a beautiful, long-lasting and successful relationship.

Grab your journal and write down a few ways that you consider yourself to be strong. Give an example of how you have used your strength in a relationship.

- How have men reacted to you when you display these attributes?

- How do men react to you when you don't display them?

- When using your strengths are you still subtle, gentle and ladylike?

- How do you think that has, or will affect your relationships?

7

Men Are Babies

HAVE YOU EVER HEARD SOMEONE REMARK THAT men are just babies? As a man, I have to admit that this statement is the absolute truth. To make things even worse, the more successful and powerful a man is the more likely he is to need little things that can make him appear to be even more like a baby to a woman. However you slice it, we are very much like babies. We have needs that only women can fulfill, we have fragile egos, need encouragement and support at home, and very much need to feel loved and appreciated. Yet, unlike babies, good men whose needs are met will provide safety, shelter, romance, security, stability, intimacy, and fulfillment to their women. They also can supply large diamonds, cars, and homes and make every woman wish she had what you have, but I know those are not things that *you're* looking for.

Good men need to provide these things, and many good men are looking for good women to provide those things for. It makes a man feel complete, and as if he is serving his purpose in this world in relation to his family.

We have come to understand, I hope, that men are looking for challenges. We also understand that each man is looking for a woman who can meet specific needs. Yet the deeper truth in that statement is that when a good man finds a woman who can meet his needs, there may be some doubt that she will be willing to meet them.

Many relationships and marriages that start out wonderfully end in misery and tears because one or both mates have chosen to stop meeting the other's needs. One thing that I am sure of is that you already know men and women have very different needs. You may already know what your needs are, and you want a good husband to fulfill your relationship and emotional needs. It is a man's responsibility and his desire to fulfill those needs for you. Similarly, it is your responsibility to fulfill your husband's needs. Yet in order fulfill the specific needs of your good man, you must first understand the needs of men in general. Of course it's true that individual men may have specific needs. For instance, some men need an organizer, some need a creative partner, some need a cook, others a pacifist, and others need an aggressive woman as a mate. Yet all men have basic *man needs* that they desire a woman to fulfill. Let's look at what these needs are, and let's understand how women sometimes misread and misunderstand them.

First, all men need respect. They need to feel honored, admired, and appreciated. They need to feel empowered to lead their families in the right directions for their future. A man without honor does not feel like a man. Only women have the power to make a man feel this way. That is why men will go to great lengths to impress and win the respect and admiration of a woman or women in general. When a woman fulfills this need and a man feels that he has admiration and respect from his woman he will fight like a lion and at all cost make sure that his family has what they both need and desire for the future. A man will work very hard to be sure a woman makes him feel like a man. Having his woman's respect gives a man emotional security. The absence of respect and admiration from a man's mate will create insecurity in that man, and cause him to search for ways to fulfill this need. If this need is not met the feeling of insecurity will become consistent, and can potentially destroy an existing and otherwise good relationship. It is also major cause for infidelity. Simple ways in our culture such as the man opening a door for a woman or ordering meals at dinner have been used to help initiate a certain divide that provided respect and honor for both the woman and the man. As our society has changed these things and other things like them may or may not exist. No substitutes have been provided by way of our ever-changing society and relationships are suffering because of changing views that re missing basic elements for a working relationship.

Always look for ways to subtly make your man feel like he is needed to protect and take care of you. If you also can appreciate his acts and respond with action (kind words, a hug a kiss) he will definitely notice, and it will enrich your relationship immensely.

Men also need understanding. Each man needs his woman to understand him as a man. Women should not expect men to think like they do or to behave as women do. A woman who embraces the differences between men and women will see her relationship work much better. A man needs his words to be listened to and understood. That does not mean that he will talk a lot, or will want to talk a lot. It does mean that the few words that he may say should be taken seriously and not ignored or talked over. If this need is not met he will often tune out emotionally, and begin to have short and seldom engaging conversations. Neglecting the need for understanding and listening can do extreme damage to the emotional connection between two people in a relationship. Having non-interactive conversation is one of the fastest ways to emotionally detach a man from a relationship.

Third, men need sex, but it has to include intimacy. Many women misunderstand this concept when they provide sex for a man who is not yet committed to them, and the result is disastrous. To a man, sex without intimacy is about as personal as eating a sandwich. You eat it because you're hungry and its fast. Not because it taste so incredible and you want to live off of it. To a man, romance is not intimacy, and commitment is. A man's version of true romance is commitment. The finality of commitment and marriage is a man's way of saying no one can satisfy him but you. In doing this he expects and anticipates his sexual needs to be fulfilled. If they are not being met it can lead to pornography, strip club visits, cheating, and even prostitute use. He truly expects joy and intimacy with his woman during sex.

Let's visit a real life story as an example of how ignored needs can affect a relationship. I have to change the names and places again to protect the innocent and the guilty, but in some circumstances there is no better teacher than real life.

John was a successful young man in the recording industry with a very high-salaried job. He loved his wife of seven years and their daughter and two sons. John was a faithful man. He never cheated on his wife, never made late night or after work visits to strip clubs, and was not a collector of pornography magazines or movies. He worked very hard for his family and even as a young married man was planning for his children's inheritance and his retirement with his wife. He was a stud who loved to exercise and it certainly showed when he took his shirt off. John's wife, Julie, stayed home with the children and drove them to and from their private school every day. She checked their homework and put them to bed. From all appearances, the family was perfect.

From John's perspective, however, he was absolutely miserable and struggled within himself on whether or not to file for divorce. His wife did not fulfill any of his three universal needs. In a conversation with me, John described his relationship with his wife by saying, "She does not respect me enough to even have a conversation with her. She interrupts me before I can complete a thought, and she does everything that I ask her to do with an attitude. She doesn't allow me to have time to relax or unwind after a ten-hour day at work, and sex with her feels like a chore."

When I asked John whether he had ever tried to talk to Julie about these issues, he said, "I've tried to, but she just changes the subject." Julie had also refused to go to back to counseling. She said that the counselor was on John's side because he was a man. After John filed for divorce, his wife asked me, "What was it that was so bad? How could he ever be miserable enough to break up our family?"

John's wife did not meet any of John's needs as a man. John constantly felt that he was treated with a lack of respect because he felt as if the communication with his wife was pointless. In spite of working extremely hard to provide a quality life for his wife and children he felt she treated him as if it the only thing that mattered was what she wanted at any particular given time. His wife would constantly belittle his attempts to communicate his feelings and dissatisfactions about the relationship by blaming his comments on him having a bad day at work or something along those lines. Battling all of these disappointments in his mind it eventually began to affect his desire to have sex with her. He no longer felt an emotional connection or intimacy with her because of the way he felt he was treated.

John loved his wife, and he desperately tried to find a way to save his failing relationship. John and his wife loved each other, and they wanted to spend their lives together, fulfilling one another's needs and realizing their dreams. What was it that went wrong in the relationship the ended it in divorce?

Was John's wife the only cause of that relationship failure? It is a possibility, but highly unlikely. Her denial of the realities in her relationship contributed, but there probably were other variables that contributed to the demise of their relationship. The real question is did John's wife have the power to save their relationship and her marriage? The answer is she absolutely did have that power. Not only did she have the power to do it, she loved her husband dearly and was devastated and shocked when he filed for divorce. Something in her life was haunting her and preventing her from recognizing and meeting the needs of her husband. Whatever it is, it made a huge contribution to the breakup of her family.

Why can an intelligent, beautiful woman who is already in a successful relationship be her own worst enemy? Was Julie a bad person and a terrible wife? I don't think so. Julie was sweet, beautiful, and smart, and John felt that she was so wonderful that he married her. Their failure was more likely a combination of Julie's lack of understanding of who her husband was as a man, and her inability to overcome personal wounds generated in previous relationships. Her unwillingness to deal with her past and present relational demons eventually robbed her of what was most important in her heart and in her life—her family.

Joyful understanding and willingness are the two most important components to maintain a successful, lasting relationship. Understanding who men are as men is as important in a successful relationship as understanding who you are as a woman, and an individual. A successful relationship takes two people with a desire to serve and understand each other. Often we approach relationships that way and then begin to regress into a more selfish state of being as time passes. Being able to understand who your man is and how he communicates his needs to you is vital to the success of any relationship you may have.

In our culture, relationships take a lot of work because many people are looking for circumstances and situations that they have fantasized about. From childhood movies, books, and television shows, a young girl who becomes a teenager has been bombarded with images of what constitutes a good man for her. Pairing that unrealistic vision with normal adolescent and puberty issues can make the teen years a source of multiple relationship wounds.

The emotional pain of mistakes made in previous relationships runs so deep that unless we take the time to deal with and overcome our mistakes and the mistakes others have made toward us, all relationships from then on will suffer for it. Knowing and understanding the realities of men will help empower your dreams to become realities. A sound relationship with the right understanding from both people is as wonderful as finding your purpose in life. You and what you can offer to your mate is part of your purpose.

The destiny of both you and your mate are tied together. How you choose to serve or not serve each other in a relationship will affect the future of each of you. It is important for us to take the time to address our personal struggles and overcome the scars that previous relationships may have left on us. The relationships we have seen with others (Parents, close friends), as well as those we have experienced first hand. This is the only way we will be able to move into a better place in our lives with the people we care most about. Your purpose and your destiny are tied together with the relationships you have and don't have.

Similar to finding your purpose in life, once you get the relationship that you want it will never seem like work. Your purpose is your power. A good woman who is in touch with her purpose and her power is a magnet for a good man.

Now is a good time to stop reading for today. You have traveled a long way in our journey toward self-knowledge, and it may be best to take a day or so to allow yourself to process all of what you have read and thought.

8

Controlling Your Atmosphere

YOU HAVE POWER AS A WOMAN, AND THAT POWER is going to help you change your life in many wonderful ways. The first action we are going to take with your power is change the air you breathe. Let me explain. If you live in a polluted environment, you can breathe, but it's not the best environment for you. Some air carries bacteria that can cause common colds and flu. Some air is stale and can cause your throat to hurt or make you develop headaches. Some toxic elements like carbon monoxide are odorless and invisible, but can even cause death if inhaled for long periods of time.

These impurities are all present in the earth's atmosphere. Different places have varying degrees of impurities. California is smoggy. New York is humid. Your area of the world has its own atmospheric conditions. What many of us have forgotten or may choose to ignore is that human environments also carry their own atmospheres. Some human atmospheres enhance personal success, while other atmospheres are likely to produce failure, hatred, insecurity, and low self-esteem. These atmospheres affect finances, careers, families, relationships, and most of all they affect you.

Some places carry the atmosphere of divorce, others for marriage; others carry an atmosphere of career above any and all relationships. The important thing is that you identify the places and people that you are around and recognize the mini culture or "atmosphere that has been created around them.

Your job, your home, and all the other places you find yourself have their own atmospheres. Atmospheres will affect you in one of two ways: good or bad. The measure for whether an atmosphere affects you in a good way or a bad way is the effects it has on you. Let's look at the relationship of Claudia and Gary to see what we can learn from them.

Claudia and Gary had been happily married for eight years. They had three children and lived in a great neighborhood on Long Island. Claudia worked from time to time, and Gary was a college professor. As Gary continued on his usual path of teaching

Claudia tried various jobs to see if one would fit the hectic schedule that comes with being a good mom. Eight years into her marriage, Claudia landed a job at a local elementary school. This job appeared to be a perfect fit. Her children were in school so she had more free time, and she also got home from work in time to help them with their homework.

Gary was happy that his wife would have a steady job with good pay and summers free. The couple was excited that they could begin saving and develop a better future for their family. They were beginning to see their dreams become realities.

Three years later, a shocking thing happened that affected their relationship and their children. Gary and Claudia separated and filed for divorce. What I didn't mention about the atmosphere of Claudia new job was that all the women who worked at the school were either divorced or single mothers. When Claudia began working, she entered an environment where good, successful relationships did not exist in the lives of her co-workers. Of the nine women who worked with her seven were divorced and the other two were single mothers with one in an abusive relationship, and the other just had a very bad outlook on life and men. This kind of environment may not have a bad effect on everyone, as many successfully married women could have worked there, and even helped there co-workers.

Yet for Claudia, this atmosphere was deadly. Being surrounded by women who continually suffered from failed relationships was a very bad atmosphere for Claudia. Unknowingly Claudia began to pick up habits, attitudes and ideas from the women at her job. Although it appeared to be a great situation to work with other professional mothers and make it home in time to help the kids with school-work, it was really a social atmosphere of negativity and bitterness. As time passed Claudia became more resentful and angry toward her husband. The time she spent with her husband and her children together became more of a chore and less of a joy. Many times people who suffer from failed relationships become habitually selfish. As she continued to work in this environment Claudia became more con-cerned with her personal desires than she was with the needs of her both her children and her husband. As he self serving attitude began to grow larger, her relationship with her husband and her children began to grow further apart. They separated after she worked three years at the school. In counseling them I recommended that they both take a look at their environments and the atmospheres they have. Claudia decided to change jobs but her and Gary were already separated, and much damage was by both of them in the relationship during those three years. After to years they are no longer separated, and both are working together to restore the intimacy and joy in loving and serving each other in their marriage.

Many women walk into environments that have atmospheres of depression, pressures to have extramarital relationships, pressure to become more selfish and other negative environments. Theses are not the type of atmospheres that are going to attract the man or the life that you desire. Unless you are a psychologist, social or youth worker whose job is to make a difference in the lives of other people I urge you to avoid negative atmospheres and environments at all cost. No amount of money is worth your family or your quality relationships. You possess the power to get away from these toxins and into a fresh, clean environment. Do not be afraid to walk away from negative friendships, relationships, jobs or other environments that have negative life damaging atmospheres. Put your power to use and embrace the change.

Much like the group of women that Claudia worked with, many women who desire fulfilling and lasting relationships are stuck in an atmosphere that destines them to remain single all their lives. This atmosphere can and will change only if you are willing take the actions to change it. Change is a guarantee in life. If we start the changes in our lives we can be much more involved in whether or not the changes are good or bad. I guarantee you that the absence of quality fulfilling relationships a person's life will not fix itself. They must step up to the mirror and embrace the reality of making changes in their lives. If you are willing to embrace change and create changes in your life, your life will most definitely change. If you are single, that will probably change. If you are unhappily married that can change. If you are with someone but not married yet, that also can change. The key is understand each other's needs and having the willingness and desire to change. This is the first step toward better and fulfilling relationships.

Change is good when you cause it to happen by yourself, and it can be even better when it's positive. Change is usually not pleasant when others impose it on you. Nevertheless, whether self-initiated or imposed by others, change is definitely a part of life. The faster we can embrace it, the quicker we can get to our destinations. Prepare your atmosphere for change by developing the willingness to initiate change in your life when it is necessary. Stop sitting around waiting for your life to change. Initiate the necessary changes in your life and watch joy and freedom make you radiant, and even more beautiful.

9

The Power You Possess

WHEN I SAY THAT YOU POSSESS POWER, I'M NOT talking about the sexual power that people say women have inside their panties. I mean real power, which comes from your mind. The ability to think about and make quality decisions that can dramatically change your life and the lives of people around you is the power I'm talking about. Many women put their power on the shelf and make decisions in their lives based on popular opinion and current style trends. This often leads to women not having a clue about why their lives are so unhappy, and why they are so far away from their personal goals and desires for their lives. When women continue in a relationship with an abusive man or when they depend on the relationships with a friend or group of friends who do not have their best interests in mind are both examples of not using your power.

The ability you have been given to think and to make quality decisions is real power. You may know about that power, but you may not know how to use it effectively, or even how to allow that power to change your life and the lives of people around you. That power is inside of you. You have the power not to be a victim or an emotional wreck, and you have the power to get control of the elements in your life that will push you toward your dreams. Your power, used well, can even help you move toward the dreams you didn't know you had, those you had forgotten about or had begun to call fantasies. Within your spirit you posses and enormous amount of power, and that power is going to change your life.

As you begin to understand the power within you, you will realize the importance of every decision you make. Let's look at how Natasha used her power to make effective decisions and the results of those decisions in her life.

Natasha, a beautiful young woman, was intelligent, creative and always well dressed. Dan, a childhood crush of hers, became interested in her at a time in her life when she began to do well for herself. Dan was both handsome and intelligent, and he was also successful financially. When he was still in college, several corporations had actively recruited him, and now, in his mid-twenties, he was earning six figures.

Natasha had been raised in less than good circumstances. Her mother was both verbally and physically abusive, and her father had rarely been at home. Natasha was determined as a child to overcome her circumstances and as she entered her second year of college Dan came into her life. She was very excited at the fact that a successful young man like Dan could really be interested in her (that type of low self esteem is a symptom of self-sickness). Natasha was both beautiful and intelligent; it would be no surprise to anyone that a successful young man would be interested in her. Yet because of her past and her feelings about herself she was very excited that he would think of her. Although Natasha was in the middle of a plan she had made for her life, focusing on education and her relationship with God, she was interrupted by Dan's unexpected interest in her.

All of Natasha's friends who knew both Dan and her told her immediately not to entertain him on a relationship level because it would be negative for her, but a good-looking, successful man like Dan was a perfect opportunity for Natasha to ignore that advice. Natasha went on to date Dan, became his girlfriend, and for several years was involved in a relationship with him that was both physically and verbally abusive and demeaning. She never finished college and still sees Dan off and on, hoping that someday they will get married.

Unfortunately we all know of people who have been involved in an abusive relationship. It is so common in our culture one may think that this type of experience is normal or even necessary. It's not! Natasha chose to follow what was familiar in her life, including being in an abusive relationship. In her youth, her mother had abused her, and her father, usually absent from the home, did nothing to intervene. Natasha repeated her mistake in choosing Dan and in staying with him.

Even in such a painful situation, Natasha still had the power to overcome her past, but she did not understand her power or use it. Everyone has a certain amount of hardship and tragedy in life. Some have more extreme situations than others, but difficulty is a part of life. Everyone has the ability to be crippled by his or her hardship or be empowered by it. Surrounding ourselves with people who will tell us we are just victims and not encourage us to take the initiative to change ourselves may give us momentary support, but it won't help us to live successful lives. Problems in life can give you the strength you need to create and maintain a healthy life, or if you allow them to they will ruin your life.

Our culture may have taught us to avoid the learning process and to embrace the momentary satisfaction. What embracing that brief satisfaction has done is prevent many people from obtaining true healing, without which a person can create a lifetime of emotional suffering. The power you have is to make the right decisions in the challenging times when you really want to have a fast solution. Your power is in your decision-making. You have the power to make the decisions that can and will change your life. Whether you want that power or not, whether you use it or not, and whether you understand it or not—you have it.

Women and men who choose not to acknowledge the power they possess in their lives consistently create bad situations for themselves and those around them. Understand the magnitude of your power, your influence, and your impact on yourself and other people. That understanding will empower you to create the life of your dreams. Understand that every decision you make involves the use of your power. Use your power wisely, and make good decisions and your life will reap the benefits of your good choices.

As you begin to understand your power, you will also begin to understand the responsibility you have to yourself and to those who love you, and who you love. A truly well balanced and successful relationship is a side effect of a well-balanced and successful life.

That life only comes through consistent quality choices. The journey inside these pages is about much more than a successful relationship. I am not talking about financial success, but success in life. Joy, peace, contentment, and love cannot be manufactured by following a set of rules or a formula to gain temporary success. Financial success may give the appearance of joy, peace, and contentment, but if you are financially successful or know someone who is, you know that the common belief that money makes you happy is very untrue. The beginning of a successful life starts and ends with you and the choices you make. Make the choice right now to embrace your power and use it wisely. Choose to value yourself more than you have in the past. You are very valuable, important and hold the keys to many good things for yourself. As a woman, you have power that no man can ever have. Use it wisely, and you are likely to have the relationship your heart desires.

Natasha chose to use her power unwisely by acting as if she didn't have any power at all. Her life of relational abuse and emotional distress will continue until she embraces her power and walks out of that abusive relationship.

A true King that's worth marrying will only partner with a true princess. A princess carries herself with dignity, honor, self-respect and purity. You have power in knowing who you are and what you stand for. You have honor, dignity, and depth when you know and understand the power you possess. You have the power to find your prince, and make him a king. Continue to get in touch with your feelings, your desires, and your true needs. As you understand your power and use it wisely, you will then begin to walk towards the things that you want and need, instead of walking away from them. Right now you are walking toward your dreams, using your power to learn and apply good principles to your life. You are choosing a wise way to use your power. Let's keep going in the same direction, and together we can watch your dreams come true.

10

Stop Wasting Time

SEEING YOUR DREAMS COME TRUE WHEN YOU BEGIN to use your power can become a reality rather than a fantasy. When you become aware of your power, be aware also that your life on earth does not last forever. Use your time well, and don't waste the time you will have to make those decisions that benefit yourself.

As an example, lets discover some truths in the life of a single young woman named Diana who had been in a relationship with her boyfriend Rob for over four years. She loved him, but she could never see herself marrying him. He was funny and good-looking, but just didn't have drive or motivation to do anything with his life. She had been with him since the age of seventeen, and was now nearly twenty-two years old. As she was about to finish college, Diana began to think about her future. She daydreamed about the joys of settling down, getting married and starting a family. She wanted to create of a family that she could be proud of and raise healthy smart children. She dreamed of raising a wonderful family and traveling the world with her husband while their kids were off in college. Diana was a metropolitan girl with a small town heart. She loved to dance, but also loved to bake and cook and watch others enjoy watch she had done for them. She was a fine catch for any young man. Rob new this, and had no desire or intentions to let her go.

At this point in hers life, Diana could have made important and life-changing decisions. Her three major choices were as follows:

- Stay with her current boyfriend and hope that one day she might meet the right man who will sweep her off of her feet and then she will know to leave Rob.
- Begin to pressure her boyfriend to ask her to marry him, although she didn't really want to be with him.
- Leave her boyfriend, and hope to find the right man.

The first point that you must understand about intimate relationships is this—if you are not married, the more time you spend with one or more wrong men, the less time you have to spend with the right man for you. In addition, spending time with wrong men will bring more baggage to your future relationship and seriously decrease your chances of ever being with the right man. Having a relationship with the wrong guy because he is cute or because you would rather be with someone than be alone is a big mistake. You could pick up so much harmful relationship baggage from the wrong man that you would ruin your relationship with the right man when you find each other.

Diana chose to stay with her boyfriend because he was convenient. He was always available, cute, dressed well and she already knew his routines. Then one day Diana met a man that she thought was just right for her. He was intelligent, good-looking, tall, funny, and responsible, and he had drive and integrity. Diana went out to dinner with him a few times when her boyfriend was busy. She really liked this new man and the way he treated her. Diana began to see a possible future and a family with this wonderful man. Diana began spending less time with her boyfriend and more time with her new interest. They started going out on dates more often, and eventually began to fall in love. Diana soon decided that she would leave her old boyfriend and planned an opportunity to tell him that she was moving on. He had suspected that she was dating someone else and became very irritable and easily angered. Although she was breaking up with him, she didn't want to hurt him because he hadn't done anything wrong to her. But before she could find the right moment to end the relationship, her new man saw Diana and her old boyfriend having lunch in a restaurant. Not thinking much of it he entered the restaurant unnoticed he overheard them arguing. As he slowed his approach and heard a comment about how they had been together for years. The new man was devastated. He left the restaurant as quietly and unnoticed as he came in the next day, the right man phoned Diana and ended their relationship for good, never returning or answering her calls.

By her own actions and choices, Diana had ruined the relationship that she waited all her life to find. She put aside the power to change her life instead of making decisions in her own best interest. She made decisions based on comfort and immediate desires rather than thinking her situation through and making quality choices. Her life and your life are important enough to take the time to think about the actions that you take. Don't allow yourself to become too busy to make good choices. Don't waste time in relationships that you see have no future in them. You are only risking your future, and temporary company is not worth a possible lifetime of loneliness. Make good choices, and stay away from futureless relationships.

I also want to increase your awareness of common ways people deal with information that encourages you to be responsible with people you spend intimate time with. I'll give two of the most common ideals I have seen. The first way is the *Variety Principle*. This is a way of thinking that says—"how can you know what you want unless you experience different things". This ideal encourages women to try intimate relationships with guys consistently, with no reason or requirement other than the basics of looks, grooming and adult toys (car, house, etc.). This is bad choice and a dangerous way of thinking. To try out relationships as if they are the latest clothing styles or food choices is juvenile and irresponsible thinking. Life does not get a dress rehearsal, so you should do your best to make the right choices in your life. People, feelings and emotions do not come off of you as easily as a pair of jeans.

The second common way that is people deal with information concerning who they spend their time with is *Selective Sense*. This is a way of thinking that says—"Before I allow myself emotion connection or intimacy with anyone, I must first find out more about this person than the surface lifestyle, looks and toys." This is a much better way of thinking because it allows the person to actually get to know someone before allowing their emotions to become attached, or physical intimacy with a person they are interested in. This greatly increases the chance of developing a satisfying relationship and emotional connection with someone. It also reduces your chances of bad and horrible experiences with individuals who on the surface where very attractive, but in reality where very close to monsters. I recommend that you be very selective in your relationship and intimacy choices. It will increase you opportunity for success in life, and make success in a relationship much sweeter and more valuable.

As you continue learning and changing, focus on using your power to make the right choices so that you can change your life for the better. Remember that your minutes, hours, days, and years are limited. Use your time to your best advantage.

11

Uncovering the Lies

THERE ARE DOZENS OF LIES ABOUT MEN. THESE LIES include stories that women tell each other that have wrong reasoning and wrong conclusions about man. The stories have been passed down for generations of women and continually ruin the understanding between the sexes and ruin any possibility of men and women accepting and respecting the vast differences between them. Think for a minute about all of the things that you believe about men in general; are they dogs? Do they only want sex? Do they not pay attention to details? There are many social beliefs about men that usually are no less than absolutely wrong. Though I cannot address all of these lies, I will address the one that is the most prevalent in our society. That is the lie that men are not sensitive. This lie, and the belief of this lie can be one of the most detrimental misconceptions in a relationship.

Men are indeed sensitive. They are affected by the attitudes, feelings, and circumstances of other people. Especially the woman they choose to be with in a serious and intimate relationship. Men are just as sensitive as women, if not even more sensitive.

This fact may be hard to accept, but it is an invaluable truth for a woman to realize and use in her relationships with men. Keep in mind that men may not cry about their feelings or tell even their closest friends about what hurts their feelings or bothers them. I speak from experience as a man when I tell you that men do have feelings, and when those feelings are hurt, men don't respond with tears, but words and action.

The key to understanding the emotions of a man is to first eliminate any assumptions you already have about those emotions. Men are very sensitive to things that women may not be sensitive to, and vice-versa. Men and women also respond very differently when their feelings are not treated with consideration or respect. Yet that is the beauty of the difference between men and women. That is why both sexes need each other, and can be incredibly influential in the others life in very positive or negative ways. We will start this next turn on our journey with a story about a man named Max.

Max was a newlywed when his first child was born. Avery excited, loving and dedicated father. He read constantly about how to educate his child better, and he spent a lot of time planning for the future of his family.

Despite his careful preparation to be an excellent father, Max realized that his beautiful wife had undergone dramatic changes after she became a mother. In our culture, a beautiful and intelligent woman may begin to feel less attractive after she has a child. Feeling unattractive, her sex drive was low, her self-esteem dropped, and her relationship with her mate began to suffer.

Max did not understand what his wife was experiencing. To him, she was beautiful and sexy when he met her, she was beautiful and sexy as a pregnant woman, and she was beautiful and sexy now as the mother of his child. He did not see a problem. Late one evening Max came home from a long, very rough day at work. Although he had been invited out for drinks with his friends, he declined the invitation because he was excited to get home, put his young child to bed, and spend time with his lovely wife. After dinner, when the baby was sleeping, Max and his wife had a few moments to themselves before they went to sleep. Max began kissing his wife who at the moment didn't appreciate his advances. She began pushing him away from her, and told him vigorously to stop. Max calmly stopped touching her and rolled over to sleep. The following day Max accepts the offer from his friends to go out for drinks after work. Max's feelings were hurt, but he neither cried nor complained to his wife about what she had done. Instead he just nodded and said to himself, "Next time, I'm going to enjoy myself before I come home."

Is this a case of Max not being sensitive to his wife's feelings or needs? She certainly thinks so.

Is this a case of his wife not being sensitive to her husband's feelings and needs? He certainly thinks so.

The truth about men is that they are proactive in dealing with their feelings. They are unlikely talk about their problems with anyone, and they won't cry about the pain or complain to their friends. What they will do is take steps to fix the problem. Men who feel rejected may begin going to strip clubs, consider having an affair, begin visiting prostitutes before they come home from work, or start a pornography collection. Many women view men's going to strip clubs and reading porno magazines as just activities that guys do. That may be the case for a teenager or a college kid to frequent strip clubs and tell sex stores as a joke. Yet usually if a mature adult male is taking regular part in those types of behaviors, it is usually a direct result of something very serious going wrong in a relationship that he has with a woman.

Men respond with action. Some men may just look at a rerun episode of "Bay Watch"; others may have an affair. Either way you as a woman can be in tune with your mate's ego and feelings, so that your relationship can be that much better and secure. Rarely will a guy share verbally what his painful feelings are, let alone allow a woman (or anyone else) to know that his feeling were hurt. This is not saying that you have to always be in the mood to keep your relationship secure. What it is suggesting is that you are very careful when handling how you express that feeling. As a woman, you have a choice: you can be in tune with your mate's feelings, or you can ignore them or remain unaware of them.

Although I used sex as an example, men's feelings are not exclusive to sex. A man's feelings are sensitive in general. I also don't want you to misinterpret the example of a married couple's sexual problem to mean that you should sleep with a man whenever he asks. Any man that is worth being with will and should respect your wishes concerning sex. Pressuring a woman for sex is not a quality of a good man. As a woman, being tactful and delicate with your words is as important to a good man as beauty, honesty, love, and companionship. In your femininity is the power to aid and empower a good man. It is everything that he needs, but doesn't have within himself. Everything that you as a woman possess your mate or spouse will need to be complete.

In your communication with your man lies the power to encourage, empower, or damage him and your relationship. So when dealing with men, you must understand that a man's sensitivity level is very high, and he will take action to defend it. It's not called our *feelings* because that sounds too delicate. It's simply called our ego. What this word ego really represents is a man's sensitive feelings and emotions.

The key part to understanding a man is getting in touch with his feelings (ego) and with the ways men protect and sustain the ego. Keep in mind that the ego affects a man's confidence, his drive to succeed, and his work ethic. Also, and most important to the topic of this book, a man's ego affects his commitment level in a relationship. So understand that if a man feels that his ego is hurt, he will respond immediately to repair and rebuild it as best he can. This is a time when a man can commit things that can be very damaging to a relationship. An excellent way to approach a man's ego is as if it were a very expensive piece of china. If handled with great care, the china can impress your friends, make dinner more beautiful, and become very valuable with age. If not handled with care it can easily be broken and become worthless or much less valuable after it is repaired. In a relationship the feelings of a man are shaped and molded by the way the woman he has chosen to be with treats and responds to him. If you can preserve his feelings you will also preserve your relationship with him. Oftentimes ego is looked at as an arrogant way of being or trying to be macho, but it simply is another word for a man's feelings. By protecting and building the ego of your man you will protect and build your relationship, and how much the man of your dreams values and respects you and his relationship with you. If you had a man who valued and guarded your feelings how important would that person and that relationship be to you?

If you have made it this far into the book you are very close to understanding realizing the power you possess to get and keep a good man.

Our example for this chapter; Max, decided to go out the next time he was invited by his friends, and when he came home, his wife and child were both sleeping. Disappointed, Max decided to come home earlier the next time and to try again to share and receive affection from his wife. As time goes by, Max and his wife are continually working to understand each other's feelings and needs, and are trying to meet them joyfully. Resolving an issue rather than ignoring it usually leads to a stronger and more fulfilling relationship. Don't look at a bad situation or intense argument as a negative. Rather look at it as an opportunity to resolve issues in your relationship for good. It can allow you to see how to create a much more fulfilling and satisfying relationship for your mate and yourself.

The story about Max may sound a bit ridiculous or exaggerated, but I assure you it is very real. Contrary to popular belief, a man's feelings in a relationship are very important. A gentle kiss and a comforted ego can be the difference between the slow destruction of a relationship and the nurturing of that relationship. It is not that she couldn't tell him not right now, but much more about the way she went about it. Like women, men need to be taken care of, encouraged, and handled gently. As a woman, you can have control of the success of your relationship. Possession of that power gives you strength that men don't have. That strength is what a man needs to receive from the woman he chooses to be with.

On national television, a married woman who was not in the presence of her husband said, "I am married to the greatest man alive." Her husband served as head of the Central Intelligence Agency, also served two terms as vice president, and one term as President of the United States. Her son also became President of the United States. I am not endorsing any type of politics whatsoever, but it is obvious to me that this is an amazing woman. She understood the fragility of a man's feelings and her power to affect the men in her family in ways that would encourage and empower them for years to come. Whoever said beside every great man is a great woman gave the understatement of our time. Every great man is only great because he is complete, and a man cannot be complete without the support, love, admiration and respect of the woman he loves. Without a woman beside him who is meeting his needs a man is only a dim shadow of his true self. There is a man who needs a woman who is just like you in order to fulfill his purpose and destiny. A good man needs you in order to become complete.

Take at least a day before reading on.

12

Creating an Atmosphere for Change

IF WE SPEND MOST OF OUR DAYS BUSY WITH WORK, children, watching television, text messaging or using the Internet, how can we find time to use in reaching our goals and making sure our needs are met? We tend to cover up our emotional problems, and find ways to cope with them rather than dealing with them and getting rid of certain issues in our lives that hold us back. We simply don't use the power that we have. Ignoring or being to lazy or afraid to use the power that you have only leads your life to be filled frustration, dissatisfaction and stress. If we possess the power to change our lives, why do our lives stay the same in so many ways?

I'm going to make the answers to this question easy for you. If you had over a billion dollars but never paid rent on your apartment, what would happen? If you had a well paying job but never went to the office, what would happen? Power means absolutely nothing if it isn't put to use. In this chapter, I'm going to explain how you can start to put this power in action and to make desired changes in your life.

I am not going to paint a perfect picture of joy, success, and realization of your dreams when you begin using your power. You are likely to find yourself outside of your comfort zone and experiencing emotional pain, annoyance, and frustration before you make your relationship dreams come true. Yet these negative aspects are a part of everyday life anyway. All of the stress and frustration we experience should result in a successful relationship and a successful life. So let's make it happen so you can watch your dreams come true.

In preparation for this growth, get out your journal or your diary. Make a list of five things in your life that you would like to change.

Now for each desired change that you listed, write down some of the actions you would have to take in order for the desired change to happen.

Beside each of those necessary actions, list the a few reasons you haven't performed those actions to get the desired changes in your life.

Now ask yourself, "Am I really ready for real change?" Regardless of what you may think right now, I believe that you are ready for real, positive, desired change. That is why you're reading this book. The way to achieve that real change is not instantaneous. It is a process. Be encouraged that you are making progress while we continue to go through this process.

Using your journal or diary again, describe the type of man you would like to have in your life. Be as specific as you can in your description without any of your attributes describing him physically at all. Listing no less than ten things and be sure to include things like what you both can enjoy together.

Add some information about the type of relationship you would like to have with this man.

Now go back and read what you wrote down about the things in your life you would like to change before reading on.

Now that you have thought about what you would like to change, read what you wrote about the type of relationship you would like to have with the man of your dreams.

Now here comes the hard part. Go back and read the rest of the actions you need to take to create the changes in your life that you would like to have.

Taking all these steps is designed to help you understand that in order to have what you want in life, you must take the actions required to get them. Doing what you have to do, in order to get what you want is a brief formula for success. The more you ignore the minor things in your life that you want to change, the more you push yourself further away from what you want in life for yourself. Your willingness and effort to change are directly linked to getting the people and things that you want in and for your life.

This is a hard lesson, but you are worth nothing less than the best things in life, and the best things in life don't come easily. Your life is too valuable for you to shrug your shoulders in defeat and sigh about habitual mediocrity. Nothing about you is mediocre. Regardless of what you may or may not have been told, you are wonderful, valuable, and worthy of the best in life. Regardless of what you may have done, or have been through, moments and events don't define who you are and what you can achieve. The way you use your power as you live daily defines who you are. You have love, desire, gifts, and much more to offer the world you live in, and a successful man who loves you more than anyone in the world.

Don't be fooled or tricked into believing you're not worth the type of man you truly desire. Your worth surely transcends your understanding. As your understanding of how important you are begins to match your true value, the world around you will definitely begin to change. Your world and your personal life will change, and your destiny for a successful relationship will be fulfilled.

This is enough reading for today. Write in your journal about some of the things you've experienced and learned during this reading session, and then pick up at the next chapter tomorrow.

13

The Reality of Self-Sickness

EARLIER WE SPOKE ABOUT WHAT I LABELED SELF-SICKNESS. I think by now you have realized that many in the Western world suffer from this emotional illness. The good news is that is that you are not at all alone. Self-sickness begins as a normal emotional phase that is a part of adolescence and growth. I cannot provide detailed information about the causes, symptoms, and treatments of self-sickness because this book is about relationships. What we will continue to discuss are the tolls that this sickness has taken on modern relationships is our society, and how to prevent and stop it.

The problem seems to be that our culture has pushed many women into a corner and forced them to carry into their adult lives the insecurity that they developed in adolescence. The result of this emotionally damaging carry-over is what I have labeled self-sickness.

If you suffer from self-sickness, you find that you are frequently not satisfied with yourself, have feelings of insecurity and unattractiveness, and often feel emotionally lost, helpless, unimportant, unloved, and devalued. Some women have these feeling periodically, but many women suffering from self-sickness walk around with those feelings most of the time. Severe self-sickness not only can cause detrimental problems in relationships, but also can prevent quality relationships from beginning.

I don't want you to confuse minor or temporary dissatisfaction with yourself with self-sickness. All of another or us at one time feel dissatisfied and find aspects of ourselves that we don't like. We usually can accept them, learn to live with them, and move on. Only when those feelings begin to affect the way we feel and interact with people on a daily basis it can begin to become harmful to our feelings of security and self worth. This is when normal everyday insecurities can develop into self-sickness. When our security and self worth are damaged, our relationships and desired relationships begin to suffer and possible cease to, or never to exist.

Adara was a beautiful petite young woman who was the middle of three sisters. She was a normal average college girl when she met a guy in class who she thought was absolutely gorgeous. She flirted with him and he asked her out for dinner and a movie. They had a good time together and went out together several more times. He would call her a few times a week and they would go out drinking, dancing or to dinner. After a short while she went to bed with him and very soon after that the calls got fewer and further between. Adara was smart and came from a very good family. She kept herself up to this point and was still a virgin as a sophomore in college. Away from home and being entertained by a good-looking young man she made a very common and very costly mistake. Frustrated and angry she confronted him with the question of where their relationship was going. Even though she didn't expect much, his reply was much less eloquent or respectful than anticipated. A young college man not thinking about anything other than his hormones had everything but her feelings on his mind.

"Your body is a little funny. You had a bit of fat on the sides and it turned me off."

Adara was devastated. Although she wanted to slap him she just shook her head and walked away calling him names under her breath. Although the real issue was that he already received what he wanted and moved on to the next girl, the damage to Adara was already done. It may not have showed at first. She cried, told her friends what a jerk he was and moved forward in school and in her life. Month's later Adara's friends began to notice Adara losing a few pounds, and becoming more conscious of what she ate and drank. Before her relationship with this young man she was ninety-two pounds. As she reached eighty-nine pounds her friends began to believe she was beginning to work out. As she reached eighty-five pounds they began to believe that she had a problem. Adara's normal insecurity was transformed into self-sickness after her encounter with this young man, and the toll of it began to create other issues in her life that affected her physically as well as emotionally. Self-Sickness is a reality that can occur in the most common of circumstances, and can have emotionally and physically damaging affects that.

I want you to take a break right now and process some of the things that we have been talking about. Perhaps make a few notes in your journal or diary. Relax and enjoy the rest of your day.

14

Getting the Strength to Change

IF YOU HAVE SPENT MOST OF YOUR LIFE (AS ALL OF US do) not valuing many of the small decisions you make, then you have not been responsible with your power. Realizing the importance of the decisions you make, and as well as the importance of the kinds of people you choose to surround yourself with, will allow your power to become clear to you. You can also begin to see the power that other people have. If you dig deeper, you may even find out how the decisions of others have indirectly and directly affected you! You may not understand what all of this means right now, but soon you will.

Power in our society is associated with many elements. Strength, money, beauty, and circle of influence are commonly associated with power. Yet with each of these associations comes a negative connotation or twist. Stubbornness, greed, and conceit are often associated with strength, money, and beauty.

I want you to understand that true power is not dependent on strength, money, or beauty. True power lies inside everyone and is born from desire, passion, and love. Martin Luther King wasn't a very big or physically strong man, and he wasn't from a rich family, and he certainly didn't have a powerful circle of influence being a black man in the south growing up in America during legalized racism. Yet he discovered his power and rallied hundreds of thousands of people together for the common cause of unity, justice, acceptance, and love. We now live in and take his one-time dream for granted. His dream of changing a nation was realized despite what appeared to be insurmountable odds.

Your dreams may not be as noble as his. You may just want to change your life or your choice in men, your job, or maybe you just want to meet and enjoy the company of a man who is right for you. Your dreams are likely to be a lot easier to achieve than changing the entire culture of a nation.

The strength and power to create change is already inside you. That strength can come to you as a result of life's challenges, such as pain, suffering, enduring and overcoming hardship. Only you really know how you have gotten your strength to change, but I know that you have it. What you may not have is the understanding that you can use it to change your life. Believing that you can accomplish your desired changes begins first with your decision to make a few changes to improve your life. If you can humble yourself long enough to say that you're not perfect and that there are things in your life that need to change, you're on your way.

Stating that you want to change is Step One. Step Two is to make the decision to change the parts of your life that you have the power to change. Step Three is taking action that is working towards those changes. Is using your strength to achieve your desired changes as easy as one, two, three? Of course not! But we can make great progress for the better in our lives when we work on changing a little, day by day. Lets look at these three steps again.

1. The desire to change.
2. The decision to change.
3. The actions of change.

Now that you know three simple steps of effective change, let's work on making simple, little changes that can make your life a whole lot better. Change usually is difficult because it alters security, familiarity, and comfort. The good aspect of change, though, is that it also alters the reality of your relationships, your joy, your success, and your life. All these important elements of your life can be different if you are willing to change. Look at and embrace change with great expectations instead of fear. That perspective will allow you to realize all of your life's dreams.

Understanding how to approach and embrace change usually lies in how you look at life—your perspective. When you change your perspective, your life changes. The way you see yourself, the way you see others, and the way you see the world all have an effect on how you choose to live. Change what you're looking at, and how you're looking at different things and—BOOM! Your life will change as well.

The strength to change lies deep inside you. Together we can shave off layers of your life that have been placed on top of you and cover who you really are inside, hindering your power to change. As an example, I'd like to share the story of Betty, an attractive and intelligent young woman who grew up in a not so fortunate social environment. As many young women receive encouragement and self esteem building blocks from their mothers and fathers at a young age Betty received exactly the opposite. Being called lazy, a liar, dumb, worthless, and that she would amount to nothing was normal everyday talk to her from her mother before she reached the age of nine. At her teenage years the verbal attack escalated to whore, ugly, stupid and useless. If Betty spoke of her dreams and hopes for a successful life, the response she would receive would be, "Who do you think you are? You'll never do that!" or "Why? What's wrong with where you are now?"

Betty loved her mother but yet hated how she was treated. Betty vowed to never be like her. After looking at the abuse that Betty took it is no surprise that as she grew into a woman, her ability to fulfill her dreams and her potential was always hindered by fear, doubt, pessimism, and insecurity instilled in Betty by the family's criticism. Betty strongly needed to be loved and accepted. In her mind, getting and keeping a good man was out of the question because deep inside she didn't believe she had anything to offer such a man. Her family life altered the perceptions of herself and her capabilities.

To get away from her family, Betty found a job when she turned sixteen. Her self-worth became linked to items she was able to purchase for herself instead of to the person she really was. She placed her highest values on objects such as shoes, clothes, handbags, belts, and the money required to buy them. In her search and desire for love and affection Betty became pregnant while in high school and eventually dropped out. Although she could have chosen to get an abortion the thought of harming a child was too painful for her. She felt she would finally have someone that she could love, and that would love her without having to deal with the lies and abuse she had received from her mother and men in her life. Soon she had a beautiful baby named Hope and finally began to feel that she could give and receive love for the first time. Little Hope was exactly that to her mother—hope.

Betty made the best from what she had and what she knew, but her life was not a fairy tale. The stress and pain of being a single teenage parent without healthy family support wore Betty down, both physically and emotionally. One day Hope made a toddlers mistake of some kind, and Betty emotionally exploded on her. As Betty screamed and yelled the look of fear and sadness on Hope's tiny face reminded Betty of her life as a little child. Betty fell to the floor and her and Hope cried together, both asking each other for forgiveness.

After putting Hope to bed that night, Betty was still riddled with guilt and shame, and she cried in the living room alone. Her daughter had no father and no security, and Betty felt that her child didn't even have the hope that her name suggested. Betty realized that in many ways she had become like her own mother. In spite of her intelligence and abilities, she was allowing her own insecurity, pain, and personal failures to prevent her from giving Hope a better life than she'd had. Feeling like a failure as a mother and a person, Betty cried and hurt like never before. At that moment, Hope walked into the room and hugged Betty tight; wiping her mother's tears with her hair. "I forgive you, Mommy, and I love you," She said.

At that moment, Betty began to accept that her life needed to change. The room didn't shake and the lightning didn't flash, but she realized that something needed to be done. She began working towards forgiving her parents and herself. She took self-responsibility for the circumstances in her life and that decision to take personal charge of and personal responsibility for her life empowered her to change. Although she would still battle with fear and insecurity it no longer had the power stop her progress, or ruin her life or the life of her daughter.

The essence of your inner strength lies in doing what benefits others as well as yourself. You don't have to go through a traumatic situation or circumstance for your begin changing your life. Right now you can come to the realization of your power and use it to change your life in ways you decide on. Understand that you have the power to make quality decisions that will shape your life in a better way. Getting your life in better shape helps others around you as well.

Hope's life became much better as her mother chose to use her power for positive change. As Betty did, you can change yourself by helping others. Taking action to help other people can help you put your own life into a more positive perspective. No matter what people around you may say or how they may feel, improving your own life and your focus benefits you and everybody around you. Spending your life worrying about your own unmet needs and unrealized dreams is simply unfulfilling and depressing.

Betty was plagued with guilt, shame and insecurity. Those things concealed the woman who she really was. Her creativity, her love for nature, reading and many other things that represented who she really is as a person were covered and blocked. She allowed her mother's unintentional abuse to paralyze her for a time, but not forever. Betty shed those layers of guilt, insecurity and shame and moved toward a better life. She confronted and forgave her mother and told her how she had felt unloved through childhood and into adulthood. Although Betty didn't get an ideal response from her mother, she was finally free. She had used her power and made a better life for both herself and her daughter. She returned to complete high school and now is happily married. She owns a beauty salon, and has two more children from her new marriage. Hope is now honors roll student, and still her mothers inspiration.

Before you continue on your journey, take a day to relax and think about the things we discussed along this part of the road. You may want to write a few things in your journal.

If we allow the pain inflicted on us by others to dictate what we think of ourselves, then the abusers have won. We can foster and nurture deep emotional wounds on ourselves by dwelling on the lies and negativity that others have told us about ourselves and what we can and cannot accomplish. This can create focus on what we don't have and will prevent us from focusing on the good parts of our lives and ourselves. Remember to allow the good areas in your life shine brightly. This will also allow you to have time to work on the bad areas and fix them up. You are valuable and worthy of creating a better life for yourself.

Lets review three important things we learned in this chapter.

1. The desire to change.
2. The decision to change.
3. The actions of change.

Gaining the strength to change involves making a firm commitment to yourself to create a better life. Guard your perspective, which is the gatekeeper for the direction your life will take. It also is the next road on our journey.

15

Changing Your Perspective

IN THE STORY OF CREATION, ADAM AND EVE WERE IN eternal bliss until they ate the fruit that opened their eyes and changed their perspective. It tells us "… the eyes of them both were opened, and they knew that they were naked" (Genesis 3:7). When their perspective changed, so did their entire world. Shame and fear were introduced in to their lives. The joy and bliss they once shared with each other was lost when they began to see the world around them differently.

Perspective is everything. When Adam and Eve's perspective changed, they began to hide, make excuses, pass the blame, and do many other things that can make a common and very poor relationship. Read it for yourself and see what you may able to learn from their relationship story. We need to work now on changing your perspective. It controls how you view and respond to your everyday world. Lets first take a look at your perspective based on the way you view yourself.

Although you may spend countless minutes during your life getting dressed or putting on make-up, how much time do you spend making the real you better? You wear make-up and certain clothes because you like them, or because of how they make you feel when you put them on, or because of the way people respond to how you look. Yet how much time do you spend fixing up the inside of yourself? Your feelings, your attitude and your self-esteem are equally as important. I'm not talking about momentarily making yourself feel better (like when you buy a new outfit) but rather actually feeling better about yourself with no aid of cars, make-up, shoes, clothes etc.

Your view of yourself is of the utmost importance to your life. We've spent a great deal of time and emotion on healing ourselves of past wounds that we felt others inflicted on us. What about the pain and suffering we have put ourselves through? Whether we would like to admit it or not, we create many of our problems. Not dealing with our own self-inflicted issues and wounds is a major cause of repeating the same situation. You could have the same problem with different men over and over again, and then you might begin to blame the problem on men, your life situation, your job, your parents, or some other supposed cause. Usually when you suffer the same wounds over and over again, it is because you have not yet dealt with the past problems you've been involved in and with the attitudes you have embraced based on your experiences.

The original source of these wounds may have been an abortion, an affair, and a poor decision that has caused you or someone you care about harm, the loss of your virginity, or a loss of dignity or respect for yourself. As a result, you may consistently lie to yourself about relationships in your life because you feel insecure and unhappy about the way you look or feel deep inside. Unresolved guilt, a violation of trust and many personal unresolved experiences can cause a ripple effect that can affect every relationship you have. That ripple can cause serious damage to the very essence of who you are and who you have aspired to be. Low self-esteem and a domino effect of bad situations and experiences in your life will come from not dealing with unpleasant realities. My dear friend, in order for that cycle to stop, you must deal with the past issues you have committed against yourself and begin the process of forgiveness and then healing. In order for us to start that process and deal with the pain, we have to go to the point of its origin. In this case the point of origin is you.

Understand that this section is not about regret and guilt, but about understanding and hope. Whatever terrible situation you may have put yourself through is a life lesson for your growth, not a testimony for your defeat. Ignoring inner guilt will produce sadness, denial, and depression. Understanding and hope can give you power and joy in life, but in order to understand your life's lessons you must visit the dark places in your past that have damaged you. We live in a culture that teaches people to avoid blame. Yet avoiding blame is also avoiding responsibility. If you don't think and accept that you have made a few really bad decisions and take responsibility for them, you're likely to start a repetition of sadness, make more poor decisions, and stay in denial of personal responsibility. I do not mean that you should afflict guilt or condemnation on yourself. Instead, I am sharing with you the benefits of taking self-responsibility for the valuable and precious life that you have. Maybe if I share some of my regrets with you, I can articulate what I am trying to express to you.

As a teenager I (like most guys) was under much pressure to have sex. The pressure was multiple: social pressure, cultural pressure, and the inner pressure I put on myself. I felt as if I was missing out on something that everybody was doing and enjoying. Like many young men having sex became a goal in my life. It may sound funny but I honestly didn't understand what sex is, and when I reached my goal, on one level I was excited and triumphant, yet on another level I felt cheated and unfulfilled. Although I had finally reached my goal, I felt depressed. Although the girl was extremely beautiful and my friends would all thought I did a great job by getting her in bed but I knew that there was definitely something that I missed. My virginity was lost, and I never would be able to get it back. Worst of all to top it off it was with someone I didn't even care about.

Like most people I didn't dwell on those thoughts at all. I quickly put them out of my mind and focused on the fact that I had reached my goal. My friends all patted me on the back and I no longer would be lying when I told people I wasn't a virgin anymore. So what happened to me after not dealing with and accepting my mistake? What else—I continued to repeat it. Over and over looking to become satisfied, but only wondering why things would never work out. I really desired a meaningful relationship, but what I pursued was sex. I, like many men actually pursued sex while what I was really looking for a meaningful and fulfilling relationship. A meaningful relationship was probably the same thing that the women that met were looking for as well. Unfortunately sex and the preoccupation with it led me pick up and drop off relational baggage that

I will carry with me for the rest of my life. Now after thirteen years of marriage, I can only wonder how much more wonderful our lives would be together if sex was what only the two of us had shared together. I can blame no one for that poor decision except myself, and I can only wonder what things I am missing out on, and hope that my children will not suffer the same fate.

I don't want to have you feel guilty or sad about any decision you have made because I feel neither guilty nor ashamed. I regret what I did, and I wish I had not done it. Yet I learned from that mistake. Love and self-understanding have allowed me to turn my mistakes into benefits for others and myself. Now I am able to properly articulate to my children how important a decision losing your virginity can be. Rather than just saying don't do it, or just tell them to protect themselves and then hope they don't fall into the fifty plus percentage of failed marriage rates we have in our culture. We don't have a rate that measures all of the pain and issues that come from failed relationships. If we did I'm sure it would be higher than fifty percent. I hope my children will make a decision based on their understanding of what sex is, what it means and what the ramifications of intercourse with another individual will do to them, rather than on social, societal, and peer pressure. I hope that for all of my readers as well.

In your diary or journal, share a detailed story of an extremely bad decision that you have made, and explain how you may have suffered from it. When I call a decision *bad*, I don't mean that it is an evil decision, but it is one that causes harm to you or to other people. Make sure you share how you felt and what you thought when you did it, and later how you felt and what you thought after it was over.

Sometimes we can get so used to our own pain that we feel empty without it. The truth is that emptiness is the right feeling to have after you rid yourself of your pain. When you go through a process of healing your wounds, you then are able to fill your life with better understanding, better people and have better experiences, and dreams. As you have shared about your mistakes and your feelings as a result of them, let's start the healing process by getting forgiveness for yourself.

A bad decision and a painful experience can cause you to remain in a state of denial that anything harmful has happened to you. Denial places you into a cycle that repeats the same situation with different people in different surroundings. Part of denial comes from not taking responsibility for your actions, part comes from not taking control of your life, and a final part comes from your lack of forgiveness towards yourself. Many times, too, guilt can manifest itself in the form of denial. Not dealing with an issue that you feel responsible for allows the superficial part of your mind to relieve you of guilt. Yet this relief is only temporary. Not working and thinking through situations in your life can cause serious repercussions.

Not working and thinking through situations in your life causes serious repercussions. Whether or not you are responsible for a particular situation is something you have to come to grips with, and get a hold on. If you are not responsible for it then you need to free yourself of that bondage of guilt. If you are responsible for it you need to correct your wrongs, seek forgiveness and move on. The pain and sufferings that come with denial and guilt will make themselves loud and clear in your life.

The first step in freeing yourself from denial and guilt is to confront your faults and mistakes. Such an honest confrontation may be a little scary, but it is much scarier to live your life fearing that misery is waiting for you. Denial and guilt don't produce positive results in your life. The negative spirit that comes with denial and guilt will keep your joy from being alive. So with that in mind, let's take the next step in gaining understanding. Let's begin to bring healing and forgiveness to ourselves.

You will need your writing tools again to climb this hill toward healing. So find a quiet place, get a pen and your journal or diary, take a deep breath, and write down some of the worst decisions you believe that you have made. Don't write down any results, just the bad decisions, and some of the reasons you made those decisions. Don't write down petty decisions such as what you ate or didn't eat, but rather major incidents in your life that you will probably never forget. After you spend a little time writing or thinking about this, move on to the next chapter.

16

The Hills of Healing

THE NEXT PART OF YOUR JOURNEY WILL BE A LITTLE brighter. We'll call it reaching the hills of healing. I think of this part as a hill because we have to climb it—not physically, but mentally and perhaps spiritually.

When you're climbing a hill, you notice that the terrain usually gets steeper as you get closer to the top. You may find that, the closer you get toward the top of the hill, the more effort you need to make. Yet the benefits of reaching the top of a hill can be understood and appreciated only by those who get there. At the top of the hill, the world looks much smaller. The problems and the situations in your life look easier to conquer, and the biggest bully in town is a mere dot on the ground. When your perspective is in its proper place, you can look through all of your options, and make the choices that lead you to joy.

The first step up this hill is receiving forgiveness. Earlier on our journey, you gave forgiveness to people that had hurt and damaged you. Now it is time for you to give this type of forgiveness for yourself. I don't know what faith you profess or even if you profess a faith, but either way it is time for you to ask God for forgiveness. Get into a comfortable place on the floor or as best you can wherever you are, and thank God for helping you to survive in spite of all that you have been through. Consult your diary or journal as you tell God all about what you wrote in your last sharing session. Be honest and open. Share your deepest pain, your deepest fears, and your deepest guilt. Just say you're sorry if you need to. God understands what you have been through and what you are going through even now, and he loves you in spite of everything and anything you have done. Ask him for forgiveness, and ask him to help you receive the forgiveness he has for you. Bow your head and start your conversation with God. Try to take at least five to ten minutes dealing with this part of your journey, and then take a few minutes to relax before you come back to the next paragraph.

Now that you're done asking for forgiveness, it's time to begin forgiving yourself. God has already forgiven you, but you still need to deal with yourself. It may seem a little awkward, but this is a very important part of our journey. Just as you did earlier when you called out loud and forgave the people who had hurt you, you must now take the time to call out loud and forgive yourself. Get yourself in front of a mirror, look yourself right in the eyes and say, "I forgive you." Continuing to look at yourself, say, "I love you," You must speak loud and clear! Speaking to yourself in this way will help you empower and free yourself through love and forgiveness. Continue to look into the mirror and say out loud "I forgive you for making decisions you knew were wrong". "I love you, I forgive you, and I will fight to do what is best for me. "Forgive me for taking the easy way out. I will work hard to do what's best, and not what is easiest for me".

Repeat this a few times. Afterward take at least a day before moving on to the next chapter.

17

The Relationship Survey

THE RELATIONSHIP SURVEY IS DESIGNED TO HELP YOU learn how feel about yourself, your ability to feel attractive, and your sense of security. This is not a pass or fail test, so please do not be nervous. All answers are correct answers because they represent your feelings and can help you to understand yourself better. As much as I care about your feelings, I refuse to share things with you without encouraging you to challenge yourself. You are a strong, intelligent woman. If your feelings and hang-ups are never challenged, you'll never grow. This book is all about progress and growth in your life, and in your relationships. I believe in you, and believe in the beauty, power, gentleness, sexiness, intelligence and attractiveness you have as a woman. You possess those things simply because you are you! You will not stay the same, and have the power to do more than conquer your wildest dreams, and deepest fears. Now grab your pen, and lets do this!

Answer each of the questions as honestly as you possibly can. The impact this exercise can have on your life will be a direct result of your honesty and willingness to share the deepest and most tender feelings in your heart.

1. How often do you feel naturally attractive?

   Never   1   2   3   4   5   6   7   8   9   10   Always

2. Do you use clothes more to cover up certain features, or enhance certain features?

   Cover up   1   2   3   4   5   6   7   8   9   10   Enhance

3. How comfortable are you with your body weight and shape?

   Hate it!   1   2   3   4   5   6   7   8   9   10   Love it!

4. How often do you leave the house without any makeup on and feel comfortable without it? This includes lipstick.)

   Never   1   2   3   4   5   6   7   8   9   10   Always

5. How comfortable are you having a conversation with a man who finds you very attractive, whom you do not find attractive?

Very uncomfortable 1 2 3 4 5 6 7 8 9 10 Comfortable

6. When was the last time you told another person that you love them?

A long time ago! 1 2 3 4 5 6 7 8 9 10 Today!

7. Do you feel that a highly successful man that you find extremely attractive (movie star/high powered lawyer/developer/) could be attracted to you?

Not at all 1 2 3 4 5 6 7 8 9 10 Definitely

8. How do you feel about being photographed?

Hate it! 1 2 3 4 5 6 7 8 9 10 Love it!

9. How intimidated are you by being exposed as wrong in any particular situation or issue?

Hurts my pride 1 2 3 4 5 6 7 8 9 10 Doesn't matter

10. How comfortable are you with yourself naked?

Not at all 1 2 3 4 5 6 7 8 9 10 Love being naked!

11. How promiscuous has your sex life been?

Very   1   2   3   4   5   6   7   8   9   10   Virgin

12. What was the longest relationship that you ever had?

Two years or more   1   2   3   4   5   6   7   8   9   10   None

13. What is your view on men and promiscuity? (Which do you believe more)

Men are all dogs   1   2   3   4   5   6   7   8   9   10   Some very promiscuous, some not at all

14. To what degree do you think that finding a good man is difficult?

Impossible   1   2   3   4   5   6   7   8   9   10   As hard as any other good thing in life

15. How reliable or committed are you about finishing most projects or goals that you've set for yourself?

Rarely finish   1   2   3   4   5   6   7   8   9   10   Always finish

16. How happy are you with your surroundings, daily routine, and finances?

Hate it!   1   2   3   4   5   6   7   8   9   10   Content with changes coming

17. Do you believe men and women generally think the same or very different?

Usually the same   1   2   3   4   5   6   7   8   9   10   Nothing alike

18. How comfortable are you with attending to and affirming the male ego of your chosen mate?

Hate the idea.   1   2   3   4   5   6   7   8   9   10   It makes me powerful.

19. Do you have any male friends?

All of my friends are guys   1   2   3   4   5   6   7   8   9   10   A nice balance of males and females

20. How comfortable are you with trusting others?

Don't trust anyone   1   2   3   4   5   6   7   8   9   10   Generally trust others.

Congratulations! If you have answered all of these questions honestly, than you have received an A on this test. Now let's take a few moments to figure out what these numbers can mean.

First, add up all of the numbers you circled for each question, and write down the total score. Then find the heading that fits your total score and read the information provided.

Total Score_____

Now let's take a look at your overall score, and go through a few things that will help you understand your feelings better, and how they affect your life and relationships.

If you scored between 20 and 119: You are doing Great! This is the category I believe that most of my readers will score. You are on the verge of achieving your dreams. You may occasionally suffer from an extremely strong struggle with your self-esteem and value. It is possible that in your understanding of how valuable and beautiful you are you deserve much more than you are actually giving yourself. You are made exactly the way you are supposed to be. You are beautiful, sexy and special, and you need to understand and accept that fact. With all of the things you may not like about yourself, there is much about you that is absolutely perfect for the man you will love.

The definition of beauty is not based on magazines and television, but on people. People are all individuals with different likes and dislikes. The good man you seek and that seeks you will look at you and sees absolute perfection in your hair, your shape, your size, your smile, and all of who you are. You are beautiful regardless of how you may feel right now, how people have treated you, or what people say. Your problem is not what or who you are, but the way you view yourself. The closer you come to understanding this, the more attractive you will feel and physically become. Don't be fooled or discouraged by anyone. People that do not understand or appreciate your value are not the company that you should keep. Staying around individuals that do not promote and create progress in your life is not healthy for you or them. They become victimizers, and you become a victim. Do not surround yourself or keep company with people who do not see your personal value, potential, and worth. Whether you have a PhD, or a GED it doesn't matter. You are beautiful and intelligent, and your life is going to get better every day. Situations and circumstances are temporary. As long as there is breath in your lungs, there is the potential for change in your life. Now you can move on to the next chapter and get ready for more great changes in your life.

If you scored between 120 and 149: You are doing great. This score reveals that you are a part of a huge group of women who understand in many ways their value and worth, but who still can at times struggle with certain key issues in life. Your moderation can be great, but at times it can make it very hard for you to make tough and necessary decisions. An inability to make and stick to certain decisions in your life can be a crucial element when trying to fulfill dreams of commitment, and true love. The good news is that your moderation also shows that you possess a certain maturity and ability to make the best of things regardless of the situation. You are on a journey that will help you discover how well you can use the wonderful abilities you have. Discovering these abilities and using them wisely is the first step in removing issues from your life. Once you deal with whatever issues you may uncover, you will realize that what lay beneath them was the realization of your dreams!

If you scored between 150 and 200: Try going back to make sure that you answered all of the questions honestly and correctly. If you have not, try this exercise again. If you have, Prince Charming is looking all over for you, so hurry and get to a place where he can find you.

18

I Hate Myself!

IS THERE ANYTHING THAT YOU HATE ABOUT YOURSELF?
There may be a lot of things about yourself that you wish to change,
especially when things are going bad, or your life isn't going well. It
may be very little you hate about yourself when things are great. Or,
you may hate a lot of things about yourself all of the time. Either
way, stress, happiness and somewhere in-between we will always find
qualities about ourselves that we don't like very much. Some things
of those qualities we have the power to change, and we have absolutely no control over other qualities. Yet sometimes what we see as
our greatest weaknesses, the qualities we dislike the most, can turn

out to be our greatest assets. Those assets have been, or will be vital to your success in life.

In your journal or diary, make a list of a few of the things that you don't like about yourself. Include no fewer than five qualities and no more than ten. Not only should you write down what it is that you don't like about yourself, but give a brief description of why you feel as you do. Make sure to include behavioral qualities as well as physical qualities. We will come back to this list later.

When I was a teenager, I went through a great number of ups and downs in feeling secure about myself. I grew up very tall and very thin. I spent most of my social life as a teenager surrounded by people who didn't share my height or body frame. I stood out in the classroom as well as at a party. I was self-conscious about my height, my weight, and almost everything else! In my way of thinking, I had no good physical assets whatsoever, I felt like an oddball who had almost no chance to fit in.

My real problem was that I hadn't learned to appreciate myself for who I was. I was busy trying to imitate life around me rather than possessing the life that I had. I remember the first day I began to appreciate my height. Another student was screaming at me in class and waving his finger at me. He was being a very typical bully. I felt a little helpless at first and didn't really respond at all. As the bully continued my embarrassment turned into frustration and I slowly stood up. At that point I realized that I was looking down at the person who was screaming at me. I remember that moment very clearly. The change in the bully's expression told me right away that being tall wasn't so bad after all.

That day I began to appreciate what I had once viewed as a weakness and a fault. I no longer complained to myself about fear of my arms being too long or being the tallest person in the room. I didn't care about my height. I found that the aspect of myself I was once ashamed of had benefits, even the potential to be cool. It was the beginning to appreciate myself for who I was. Whether you're tall, short, thin or healthy there are benefits to who you are that people who are not like you don't have. You must embrace who you are and experience the freedom and love there is in loving yourself.

Now you may say that's a terrible story because everybody wants to be tall and thinks it's wonderful to be tall, but I will tell you that is not the way many tall people feel. Actually many tall individuals slouch over a bit while walking or standing in order to make themselves appear shorter. I've done it before, and I see others do it also. What is sexy, attractive and accepted as good and bad is very much related to you're culture and surroundings. In suburban American areas, many women strive to be and are under great pressure to be very thin, whereas in urban American areas, many women strive to be thicker and more voluptuous. In reality, the saying that "The grass is always greener on the other side of the fence" plays itself out in the lives of people every day. Tall people want to be shorter, short people want to be taller, slender people want to be a bit bigger (or sometimes a bit smaller), larger people want to be smaller, and so on.

One serious problem is that in our culture, we tend not to deal with adolescents' feelings of insecurity. Our society chooses instead to make money from that insecurity. The market offers weight loss and weight gain products, body-shaping tools, exercise videotapes, gym memberships, and fat free, low fat, and high calorie foods. Diet programs that focus on calories or carbs or whatever else they can use to make people feel like they can make themselves better. The result is that our childhood concerns about self-awareness develop into low self-esteem that dominates our adult lives, thoughts, and wallets. To become truly better looking or just a better person it starts on the inside. In order for change to take place you need inspiration, motivation, confidence, dreams, goals, determination, focus and peace. These are the things that make a persons life better. When those key elements are missing contentment, self-esteem, drive, control over your weight and many other things will just go on vacation. Calories don't change your weight as much as your attitude and motivation does.

How can we overcome the intense battle while we are living in a society where self-sickness is being affirmed and perpetuated? A fresh new life, energy and new attitudes are growing in your heart. The intense feelings of discontent and sadness will be running as far as it can get away from you! You are attractive, valuable, and intelligent and that you have much to offer not only a man, but also the world around you. Your beauty and worth transcend what you think about yourself, and as you get in touch with that truth, your life will begin change dramatically and your destiny of joy we begin to become fulfilled.

As a young adult I remember a group of girls (friends of my wife) who always teased the younger sister of one of the more popular girl in their group. The younger sister was tall, awkward, had very large feet and wasn't able to manage her hair well. She grew up being the on the wrong end of jokes and constantly being left out of her older sisters activities. I felt compassion for her because I also knew what it was like to grow up a tall teen and not understand how to carry your height well. Six years later my wife and I went to a wedding that had one of the most beautiful brides I had ever seen, and it was the younger sister. She had grown up to become absolutely gorgeous.

I'm pretty sure she's still the sweet and wonderful person that she always has been. Yet her perceived faults and insecurities were overcome, and she was no longer hiding or attempting to hide the things about her that made her special and different from her sister and her sister's friends. Her height, hair texture and humility made her one of the most sought-after women in New York, and she married very well. I know her story sounds like a classic ugly duckling tale, but it is a true and I believe very common story. That story is told not to suggest that all ugly people will turn out to be beautiful, but that all people can be beautiful if they get in touch with and begin to appreciate the qualities of themselves that make them unique and different from the people that they are around. Your perceived weaknesses can become your most desirable attributes if you embrace who you are with joy, love and dignity.

Earlier in this chapter, I asked you to list some of your perceived faults. Go back to your list and think about what benefits or assets are in those qualities that seem to be faults. Did it make you more compassionate towards others? Does it make you stand out in a crowd? Take your time, and consider each one individually. Then write a few things that you think are good or positive about each one.

Don't give up on this important part of our journey. It will be easy to tell yourself that there is nothing good about these qualities.

It will also be easy to feel sad and give up. But remember, we have come a long way. I believe in your ability to view your former faults as valuable aspects of yourself, You will finish this journey and be more prepared to arrive at your destination of developing a well-balanced, secure, loving, and satisfying relationship.

After you have written all the benefits you can think of for each fault, look at each fault again and write some ways that what looks like a fault might have had a positive effect on your life. It could have made you a more understanding person, given you insight to help someone else, offered you an opportunity to develop a much stronger character, or even made you more competent in other areas of your life. Whatever the case is, write it in your journal or diary. Please find a quiet place where you feel secure. Honesty on this journey is very important, and you have to be confident and comfortable that you are going to be and feel secure as you walk through this part of your journey. Only then will you feel free to share your deepest and most trusted feelings about yourself. Your security is not only important to me, but it is even more important to you. Get into a comfortable place, grab your journal and begin. After you are done it may be better move on to the next paragraph the following day.

Now that we have dealt with some of the things that you perceive as faults, let's look at some of your strengths. What you previously may have perceived as your weaknesses now have an opportunity to become additional strengths. As this happens, the scale of your life will become more balanced, and you will be a few steps closer to your destination.

In considering your perceived strengths, open your journal again and list a few qualities that you like about yourself. You should list at least five qualities and not more than ten.

Read that list again. On balance, I hope you realize that you have special qualities that should be recognized. Nobody is perfect, but as all people do, you have a lot to offer in a relationship. There is a man who needs exactly what you have. What you have and who you are will make him feel lucky, and that he found something great that every other man has missed out on. In spite of your faults and your failures you are a success. That success does not come from not making mistakes and having a perfect and wonderful life, but from learning from your mistakes—and also from the mistakes of others. You have confronted your fears, your insecurities, your past and your dreams. You have even taken the time to confront yourself. You have come a long way through this journey, continue to look forward as you become more radiant and beautiful than ever.

19

Sorting Out the Differences

I HOPE YOU HAD ENOUGH RELAXING TIME TO PROCESS what we've been going through in the last few chapters. We are approaching the last few segments of our journey, and I want you to be fresh and ready to go.

As people grow older, many of them seem to have a less clear understanding of the opposite sex, especially when they are in a relationship. It appears to be very easy to know someone when in reality you don't know the person well at all. Our minds are flooded with superficial information about people from gossip columns, talk shows, magazines, and broadcast media, but real life and real people are much more complex than a news column, headline or a talk show can indicate.

My point is that as we grow up watching and experiencing television and other forms of media, we tend not to understand it affects us, and our perceptions of other people. Yet what we think or expect as normal is based only on what we see, hear, and experience. So this allows us to understand that the information that we feed ourselves through entertaining and informative media and television affect out perceptions of normalcy realism in relationships.

How would you complete the sentence "A normal couple should …"? The way you finish that sentence is based on your experiences as a child and an adult combined with the aspirations and dreams that have come out of those experiences. Almost every person in the world will fill in that blank a different way. So what happens when you like a person, are in love with a person, or are married to a person who has that blank space completed very differently from the way you completed it? As you may imagine, confusion, stress, frustration, and struggles begin. Generally, people have not learned to understand, value, and appreciate other attitudes toward life. Because we have not learned to accept others' (Spouse, boyfriend/girlfriend etc.) ideals of living, we may attempt to force our companions or potential companions to conform to our way, or get frustrated and unhappy while attempting to change the companion.

The selfishness that we begin to experience often causes us to value fantasy-filled relationships or the expectation of a relationship that is essentially a fantasy. Seeking only a tall, intelligent, good-looking man who dresses well, makes a great deal of money, is well educated, has a great job, doesn't fart around you, likes to cook and clean, is from the race or background we want, doesn't scratch himself and loves us no matter how we change physically over time is relatively unrealistic. That person is closer to a cartoon character than he is to an above average man. Setting standards and having expectations is fine, and actually important. What is equally important and really even more important than having standards, is that your standards must be rooted in qualities that create and help maintain a successful relationship, and not just qualities that create the appearance of a wonderful and successful relationship.

Balancing what you need emotionally, with what you desire superficially is the key in your search for the right man. What are those deep, real, need-based qualities? What many women really want is a man who is attractive to them and who can be trusted. They want a man who will provide security and stability for them both emotionally and financially. Yet many women spend time looking for a handsome man who makes them feel comfortable and proud around their friends and family. This often allows them to unconsciously sacrifice important basic necessities such as trust, consistent responsibility, future vision etc ... This typically creates trouble further into the relationship when they must inevitably cope with issues and pressures that will occur in a normal relationship: Finding a balance between your desires and your real needs are important in getting yourself in the right frame of mind for getting and keeping the right man.

20

The Destined Single

WHEN A PRETTY AND SUCCESSFUL WOMAN WHO desires a meaningful relationship is not found attractive to or by men for a serious relationship over a very long period of time is a simple explanation for a complex problem called *the destined single*. Most women know at least one destined single, and many women are afraid that they may be destined singles themselves. The term *destined single* doesn't have a nice ring to it, but the destined single has become more and more prevalent in our modern society. What is a destined single? Who is she? What does she look like? How can a person tell if she fits into this group? I'll answer all of these questions in this chapter.

What is a destined single? A destined single is not a woman who chooses her career over her relationships or a woman who is aggressive, active, or athletic. A destined single can be a woman who longs for a meaningful relationship with the opposite sex, but for some reason that neither she nor any of her friends understand, that meaningful relationship has not come close to happening. She usually is very physically attractive and constantly receives questions about why she is alone.

A girlfriend of mine had an unusual group of about five good-looking friends with whom she grew up. Unusually it was a group of several very pretty girls hanging out together. We were all in college students between the ages of nineteen and twenty-one. Many of my friends went out or attempted to go out with almost every one of my girlfriend's friends, who were all very attractive. After getting to know each of these beautiful young women as friends, I told my girlfriend that one of her friends, whom I will call Dawn, would be single for the rest of her life.

My girlfriend scolded me at the time for saying such a thing and said that I was being mean, though I really was not. After spending consistent small amounts of time with Dawn it was clear to me that no man would ever desire to spend their life with her. My girlfriend still felt that somehow I was being cruel or that Dawn had offended me and I was retaliating but that was very far from the truth. I actually thought that Dawn was a very nice person, and she was beautiful. Sixteen years later, Dawn is still single and has no boyfriend, nor has she had a boyfriend since college (and actually before college). To make this real life story even more bizarre, the truth is that when the average guy sees Dawn, he thinks that she is very attractive. Dawn is a very nice woman who sincerely desires a meaningful relationship. So what exactly are her problems, and the problems of women like her?

I have mentioned that Dawn is physically attractive. If that is the case, what does a woman who is destined to be single look like? There is no physical description or attribute that is always characteristic of a woman who is a destined single. Bearded women have husbands, as well as women of all shapes and sizes. A woman who unknowingly destines herself to be single can be physically attractive, dress great, have a good job, and be intelligent. None of those qualities have the power to pull her out of her single status. There are common attributes of a mindset that can place a woman into a destined single status. The key attribute in developing this trait is leaving undesirable aspects of your life to reside in a state of denial and emotional block. This prevents many women from accepting self-responsibility for their own situations. They are convinced in their own minds that their single status has nothing to do with them. Usually they attribute their single status to bad men or stupid men, or ideas that all men are dogs or that all the good men are taken. At one time or another many women may have expressed these common sentiments but the difference between an average woman and a destined single is that the destined single actually has convinced herself that these are the reasons she is single. The destined single is convinced that she knows exactly what kind of man she wants, thinks he exist somewhere on earth and she is just waiting around for him to show up.

This information may sound harsh or insensitive but nevertheless it is a reality that is important for you to understand. It can help you as well as people you love in dealing with and understanding issues that may prevent them from living a full and more satisfying life.

What was it about Dawn that has her fifteen years strong without a second date? Simply put, it was her confidence in the wrong attitudes and ideas that had come from never dealing with the mistakes of her past. Regardless of the negative results of her past decisions, she continued to blame others for her problems. Her behavior demonstrated chronic denial, and that is an instant turnoff for men of all ages who are interested in a serious relationship.

There are though, several very simple things that can be done to help her and many other come out of destined singleness. Most of the hard-pressed issues of life's past that Dawn struggled with we have dealt with in the earlier chapters. So lets deal with the other important but lighter things that every woman should know about getting and keeping a good and even a great man.

First, every man wants a wife who satisfies certain needs for him. All men have similar needs. Some needs are more important than others, and each man will weigh his needs according to his personal issues and preferences. In an earlier chapter, I discussed three basic needs that all men have—respect, understanding, and sex. Now I want to talk about other needs that may seem rather small, but can be extremely important in a meaningful and worthwhile relationship.

First, a woman should be fun. Just as a woman wants a man she can have fun with, a man wants a woman who is fun, who has enthusiasm and who smiles easily. Enthusiasm and smiling are contagious. A woman who loves to smile is always more beautiful and attractive. Relaxing and being able to have fun without being self-conscious is a sure way to attract a good, hard-working man. Men who work hard need a woman to relax with and to get their minds off the pressures of work. Nothing can be better than a lighthearted woman who can have fun sitting quietly in the park or going mountain climbing. I give those two extremes to make an example. A woman that can find fun and joy in situations that she is not used to and willing to try new things is much more desirable than one who is stiff, afraid or annoyed at trying or being exposed to something new. Having fun doesn't mean getting on a rollercoaster or skydiving, but it does represent trying new things with someone and creating new and memorable moments by doing something together with someone. To be a desirable companion, learn to get more comfortable with exposing yourself to new things, relax, create some memories, and have some fun.

Second, as we have discussed, men are babies and need a lot of attention. A woman who is attentive to a man is guaranteed to attract more men, and if she has a man it will definitely make their relationship more secure. Gaining a woman's attention is the most basic and natural instinct that a man has. It is something that men do. A woman who is attentive to a man's needs when he is not looking for attention. Let me give you a few examples on this one because it is very important. Lets create a common mental picture of a young couple, happily in love on a Monday nigh after work. They have finished eating and the man is sitting on the couch watching sports (he could be at a computer or at his work desk, but for the sake of simplicity lets say he is sitting in front of the television) and the woman comes over to ask him a question. She says "This girl Sarah who works at my office did something really stupid today." If the man's head does not turn away from the television, computer etc., that usually means it is not a good time to attempt to develop a serious or important conversation unless there is an emergency. That does not mean that whatever he is doing is more important than you at the time, but his response is saying non-verbally that this is not the best time for the conversation. A man who loves or deeply cares about a woman wants to give her undivided attention. This is very important to all good men, yet in order to do that they must have the opportunity to get into the right mindset in order to do that. For some men it is sports, for others cards, and for some it can be work. Either way a woman who recognizes these needs is much more valuable and attractive to a man. It can be a gesture as simple as waiting until a commercial before asking a question. These simple and seemingly petty examples are small things that can be greatly appreciated by men. They may not verbally thank you for it. Yet it can make the difference between coming home to watch the game and going out to watch the game. It can make the difference between working late, and working from home. These instances over time can make huge differences in relationships. A man who loves you would rather work from home, and watch the game from home if he believes he can concentrate and get whatever he needs out of what he is doing. You are wonderful and special. You presence alone is something that a good man longs for. Even when he is busy doing other things, the thought of you, the sight of you and even the smell of you can make his life that much more wonderful. Give your good man the attention he needs, and he will never desire to leave your side.

Third, a woman should be sexy. Don't confuse being sexy with having sex. Being sexy is much more than that. In a previous chapter I listed sex as one of man's basic needs so that we have already covered. Being sexy is behavior that transcends the bedroom. A sexy, appealing woman has a lot to offer a man in a relationship because she fulfills his desire to have a continually appealing companion. A woman can be sexy in many ways. Her clothing, touches, looks, intelligence, and attitude all combine to make her a sexy person. And I have yet to meet a man who doesn't want such a woman.

Ladies, be very careful with this need. If being sexy is an aura or a persona that you show during courtship, you must be willing to continue it throughout your relationship. Don't be a sexy, beautifully dressed girlfriend and then get married and walk around in an old blue T-shirt. Don't overdo sexiness when you are seeking a partner or dating a man. My advice is to leave the sexiness for your marriage and your lifelong mate. If you are fun, attentive and meet a man's needs you will have a lifetime with that man to be as sexy as you want to be.

Now that we have discussed these important attributes of a woman, lets look at a few common things some women do that discourage men from considering them as partners? Behavior such as talking too much and being more concerned with their own needs much more than the needs of their man is almost certain to lead a woman to single status. A good man desires to meet his women's needs, when his mate is more concerned with her own needs rather than his a man is forced to do one of two things. His first choice is to attempt to meet his own needs in hope that his mate will soon meet them. His other choice is to give attention to another woman who is trying to get his attention and meet his needs. His desire though, is that the woman he is with meets his needs. If that happens a good man will be willing to do anything he can in order to keep that woman happy, satisfied and well taken care of for the future.

A good man who finds you adorable, intelligent and sexy will find you. When he does arrive, be ready for him, and don't accidentally send him away to look for another partner. Engage the opposite sex in conversation, in dinner, in a movie, or in any situation where you feel comfortable and unthreatened. A man doesn't have to be your husband or a future husband. All he has to be is a nice, decent person. Don't substitute person-to-person encounters with waiting for the perfect situation, or the perfect man. Enjoy Even if he is not the right one for you, enjoy life, and enjoy the company of others.

21

Exposing Relational Fantasy

WHAT I CALL RELATIONAL FANTASY IS THE SAME IDEA
that storybooks describe by saying, "And they lived happily ever after."
This type of relational fantasy starts in our minds and slowly makes
its way into our expectations. When it takes refuge in our attitudes
and actions, relational fantasy begins to destroy our relationships.

The misconception of two people's being in happiness and
bliss forever in a relationship has proved itself detrimental to relationships and the understanding of them. The divorce rate seems to
increase continually regardless of the financial or occupational success of the family. A self-centered search for eternal bliss and comfort
lies deep within our hearts, and we seek it out in our relationships.

That search can lead only to constant frustration and "relationship surfing, a behavior in which people hop from one relationship to another. The bliss of true happiness in life can be found in fulfilling your purpose, not in fulfilling your immediate relationship and emotional needs.

Fulfilling your purpose will not happen by chance or fate. Fulfilling your purpose lies is your willingness to work hard and not give up on your aspirations and goals in life as well as in your relationships. Finding the right man for you is a part of your destination in life, and fulfilling his and your life through that relationship is a part of your purpose. You are likely to develop a successful relationship if you are willing to take all the actions needed to create and maintain it.

Relational fantasy lies in the heart of everyone, but the superior sensitivity level of women's minds makes them more vulnerable to this type of outlook. From *Romeo and Juliet, Cinderella,* and *My Fair Lady* to *Pretty Woman* and *Maid in Manhattan*, our society has capitalized from this sensitivity of women. Yet relational fantasy leads to unrealistic expectations and ideas, and the breakdown of initially successful relationships.

What many women expect, secretly desire, embrace, and are romanced by are not qualities of honesty, integrity, commitment, security, and love. What many women look for and expect is very much to the contrary. Style, manners, appearance, and charm and other Prince Charming qualities can be sexy for a while, but that have little to do with a successful relationship. It's no coincidence that rarely do individuals marry from their first relationship, and yet and still over half of marriages end in divorce.

Not taking the time to care for a valuable item causes it to become neglected and nonfunctional. In this case the valuable item is your life and your relationship with your chosen man. Let go of the unrealistic attitudes, expectations, and actions that have previously not given you success in your relationships. Letting some of these things go can be uncomfortable and painful. Often in life pain can be the prerequisite for success and greatness. The pain of missing a few parties' results in better grades, the pain of childbirth brings forth a beautiful child. Get and stay excited about enduring and addressing certain hardships and pain that may push you out of your comfort zone, but closer to your destiny of a wonderful and fulfilling relationship.

22

Breaking the Cycle

THERE IS A CLICHÉ THAT SAYS, "IT'S NOT THAT PEOPLE plan to fail, they just fail to plan." That statement holds more truth than many understand. For your life, and your relationships, planning is very important. Yet our society teaches us that when it comes to relationships, learn by experience. What we really learn is how to create relationships that fail, and in that we fill our lives with more emotional and relationship scars.

What does it take to break the cycle of relationship failure in life? Let me encourage you to try to break the cycle because succeeding takes a lot less effort than you might imagine! All it takes is a determined mind. A mind that is unmoved by the advice of television experts, friends and family, popular magazine articles, and the person you fell in lust with at first sight. A determined mind is necessary to break the vicious cycle of relationship failure that many women are trapped in. Making up your mind is very difficult in our society because we have been conditioned to avoid blame and responsibility. Whether it is a chemical imbalance, our childhood or a result of too much drinking we have been conditioned to pass responsibility rather than accept it. So if you go through life unsure about choices you have made and actions you have taken, you are encouraged to blame someone or something else for your failure. In effect, you relieve yourself of the acceptance of failure and the responsibility for making the wrong decision.

By adopting that mental stance of being unsure, you have turned your life over to circumstances. Until you're willing to be confident and secure about your choices and actions, you will continue to live burdened by the beliefs and recommendations of your surroundings and your culture. Once you can adopt the posture of certainty, you are on the surest road to your destination—even if a choice you make or an action you take turns out to be a mistake. Once you have embraced responsibility, you have the power to correct your mistakes rather than be defined by them.

You must also overcome fears of being an individual or different. Many of us spend our lives trying to fit in and to be like everybody else. We pick a style that we see other people use and then adopt it for ourselves. The style could be conservative, grunge, urban, hip-hop, yuppie, business, flashy, or almost anything else. Your struggle in breaking the cycle of relationship failure involves accepting and embracing who you, regardless of all of these outside influences.

As this journey helps you to determine and accept who you are, you should be able to reach certainty about these five aspects of yourself:

1. Certainty that you want to change in order to get what you want

2. Certainty that you are willing to keep doing the actions and making the decisions that will help you to get what you want even when you feel discouraged

3. Certainty that you are valuable enough to be loved and worthy of loving someone else

4. Certainty that no matter what anyone else says or does, you will stick to your plans until you complete them

5. Certainty that the reason you are alive is to fulfill a purpose that will positively impact and benefit the lives of other people, and especially those around you.

Your future is in your hands. Make a decision right now to refuse to live your life without fulfilling your purpose. Once you make that decision, you will be one step closer to finding out what the purpose is for your life, and fulfilling that purpose.

Enduring criticism and condemnation about decisions you have made is a big part of being certain about those decisions. Take a few moments to think about what being certain means and how that might affect you and your life. Then ask God to help you endure what you will have to do so that you may reach certainty and endure what it comes with. Also ask for the bigger picture and purpose for your life to become revealed to you. Your purpose and your destiny is filled with greatness in ways that are specifically designed for you. Find your purpose.

23

Destiny versus Dreams

ARE YOU READY TO FIND AND GET THE MAN YOU WANT, or do you want the man of your dreams? As we have discussed in chapter 19, no doubt many women would choose a tall, intelligent, good-looking man who dresses well, is educated and has a great job, doesn't fart in front of you, likes to cook and clean, is from a desired race or background, and will love the woman no matter what. Suppose you could have a man just like that. Would you want him? If you do, you can have him at any moment! Just as you did in elementary school, check one of the boxes below:

☐   Yes, I want a man just like this.

☐   No, I do not want a man just like this.

If you checked the box saying that you do want that man, get ready for some vital information. If you checked no, keep reading as well. If you didn't check either box, go back and check one of them. If you don't have a pen with you, scratch a choice in with your fingernail. Whatever you do, don't be afraid to be sure! Check a box!

If you checked yes, you might be asking where you can find this man and how you can get him. That answer is easy. He is all over the place, he is looking for you, and getting him is easy. But before I tell you how to get him, let me tell you a little more about this man.

None of the qualities you chose for him will have any lasting merit for a relationship. His qualities did not include honesty, faithfulness, ability to commit to his wife and family, loving, monogamous, respectful of women, good problem solver, or even a good sense of humor. This man may very well have been the man of your dreams, but what you really want you deserve, and it is very different, and much more than that. If you want a relationship that is more meaningful, you have to look for qualities that are meaningful in a relationship.

If you chose yes, you still made a choice because, at least for a moment, you were certain of what you wanted. The good part about being sure is that it enables you to learn from your mistakes.

Being unsure allows you to blame your mistakes on circumstances or situations. I hope in this instance you learned to look deeper at the qualities of a man that you think you want and are important. Understanding what you really want will empower you to get it.

Now let's put this learning into action. Let's start by making a new list of desired qualities in a man. This time, truly think through each quality before you write it down. Also, put your desired qualities in order of their importance to you. I will help you by suggesting a few qualities that I think a good man possesses. You can use some of these qualities and add your own, if you like.

Here is my list of desirable qualities for a good man. My qualities are not in any particular order, but you will place the most important qualities to you at the top of your list.

- He is a man of integrity and sticks to his word.
- He is an honest man.
- He loves children.
- He believes strongly in monogamy.
- He is willing to wait to have sex with you.
- He is intelligent and well educated.
- He has a sense of direction and purpose for his life.
- He is not afraid of making a commitment.
- He is loving and affectionate.

- He is a hard workingman.

- He respects women.

A quality that I also consider important—and I suspect you do, too—is that the man is not currently married to someone else!

As you look over my list and finish your own list, I hope you see changes in what you want after you've given the matter some thought. Now that you're considering the qualities required for a really good relationship with a good man, you probably see a difference in your understanding of what you want now as compared to what you may have wanted before you began this journey. Think about what those differences are and why you think you have made them. You may want to write about those differences in your journal or diary so you can keep them in mind. You do not have to make all of the changes now or write down everything you're thinking at this time. Yet it may be wise to continue to give the matter thought continually as you decide what qualities you want in a man.

Our journey together is almost complete, and if you look closely, you can see the top of the mountain we have set as our goal. The culmination of all of the changes and emotions you have experienced on this journey is about to bring you to the place you need to be. Let's keep our eyes forward, and press on to the top of the mountain.

23. Destiny versus Dreams

24

Ready to Get Him!

FIRST OF ALL, IF YOU ARE SKIPPING AHEAD TO READ THIS without reading the rest of this book first, stop! Reading the last few pages of this journey will get you nowhere beyond exactly where you are now. So if this is what you are doing, close the book and start from the beginning. I hope you will approach this book and your life with the diligence and respect they both deserve. You are valuable and your life and relationships deserve more attention than just skimming through a book that you think might help you. Start at the beginning, read every page, write the journal or diary entries thoughtfully, and watch your life begin to change.

This is a very exciting part of the journey for me because you have been through a tremendous amount up to this point, and success is just a step away. Gather your diary or journal and a pen, and let's go!

25

The Finish Line

THE FIRST TASK WE HAVE TO DO IS GO OVER A FEW things that we have learned along this journey. It is important that we look at the places we have been in life and then decide whether we want to go back to any of those places. If we do not take the time to look at where we've been, we might end up in a place we don't want to be, one that is likely to be where we've been in the past—like a poor relationship or an abusive one.

Lets review the places in the past that we visited on our journey, and consider what we have learned from our revisits to the past. Revisiting those places can help you to sort out the changes that you have made and the changes that you will continue to make in your life.

In your journal or diary, think about and comment on each of these questions:

- In the past, how has the relationship or lack of relationship with your father affected your outlook on men and your relationships with men?

- In looking at how you've felt in the past, how do you think your feelings have changed or need to change to allow you to develop a loving, trusting relationship with a good man?

- Are you willing to make those necessary changes?

The exercises that you have completed on this journey, and the experiences you have shared, and the emotions and memories you have revisited don't disappear overnight. Remember to keep this book. You should go through the exercises in chapter 4, "Cleaning the Wounds," on a regular basis. Make the mirror exercises a part of your daily, weekly or monthly routine. Remind yourself of how precious you are, what you have overcome, and where you are going. Life, much like this book is a journey. Enjoy it, and make progress in your life as much as you can.

Part of any successful relationship is understanding and maturity concerning self-change. Change is the only thing in life that is guaranteed. You will continue to change in one way or another almost every day. Your body will change, your skin will change, and your experiences will change.

A relationship always involves change. It can bring fulfillment in areas of your life that are not fulfilled. It can bring companionship, security, warmth, stability, love, joy, a family, and a host of other exciting and beneficial things into your life. Yet all these elements involve change. These changes can affect your mind, your body, your emotions, and your actions.

To fight against change is a direct contradiction of who you are as a human being and as a woman. Change is inevitable. As you embrace change, you will embrace your future, your purpose and your destiny. In your future lies the possibility of a relationship that is even better than you can imagine. Look at that possibility, embrace the necessary changes in your life, and you will make your existing relationship much better or will be empowered to develop the relationship that is right for you.

Go back and read all that you have shared with me and with yourself on this journey. Pray and learn to continually deal with and address your issues. You don't want to carry extra baggage into your next or soon to be successful relationship.

As you have been preparing yourself to be an ordinary person who has an extraordinary relationship, there is a man preparing himself for the same. Be prepared because the opportunity for the right relationship with a good man is looking hard for you. Keep in mind that success results when preparation meets opportunity. Don't continue to hide yourself inside your own feelings. You don't want to carry your baggage into your new, successful relationship. Carefully remove the baggage of your past concerns, and remember that you are extremely valuable and have much to offer in a relationship. I believe in you, and you believe in yourself. Discover your purpose, fulfill your destiny and live out your dreams.

978-0-595-36518-0
0-595-36518-3

Printed in the United States
97555LV00007B/19-36/A

9 780595 365180